"*The Twist in* ship, and devotion on many levels. Bob Hanlon has written a detailed account of the challenges that he, as well as he and his wife, Sharon, have encountered. Their lives are a confirmation of the power of prayer and the existence of miracles. Bob even includes the Danny Thomas treacle cutter at the perfect time, for even in the worst of times, he and Sharon were able to find humor."

- Nancy "Niki" Simpson
English Department Chair and Dean of
Students–Holy Innocents' Episcopal School,
Atlanta, GA

"*The Twist in the Road* is a 'must read' for any person seeking insight into acquiring quality health care as well as learning how to live their lives with strong faith and values, all the while keeping a sense of humor. Anyone considering a career in the health care field would benefit from the ideas Bob has shared, as they would see things from the patient's perspective, allowing them to work with kindness, compassion, dedication, and motivation.

Over the years I have described Bob in *many* ways, but after reading this book I would use three adjectives: loving, intelligent, and fun. I loved reading this book, and I love the fact that Bob is sharing his and Sharon's story so that many others may become better stewards as they live their lives."

- Dr. Margie Roos, PT, DPT,
NCS–Physical Therapist

"Bob Hanlon's high school years at Archmere Academy were marked by growth in academics and spirituality, true to Archmere's motto: *Pietate et Scientia*. His book, *The Twist in the Road,* allows his piety to shine forth through what he has learned and suffered. I am proud and humbled to have been one of his teachers 'along the way'."

- Father Joseph McLaughlin
Headmaster–Archmere Academy, Claymont, DE

"A true story of triumph over tragedy, *The Twist in the Road* is a remarkable tale of how faith, love, courage, and family values can make all the difference. It is a book that will make you sad and warm your heart at the same time, and it will show you how perseverance in the face of not one but two medical calamities can lead to an amazing recovery against the odds. You will learn from the book. When finished, you will feel as if you know this couple and wish you really did!"

- Dr. Greg Higbee–Emergency Room
Physician, Bryn Mawr, PA

the twist in

the Road

the twist in

the Road

*and a few things we have
learned along the way*

*foreword by:
Sharon Hanlon*

Bob Hanlon

TATE PUBLISHING *& Enterprises*

Published by Tate Publishing & Enterprises, LLC
127 E. Trade Center Terrace | Mustang, Oklahoma 73064 USA
1.888.361.9473 | www.tatepublishing.com

Tate Publishing is committed to excellence in the publishing industry. The company reflects the philosophy established by the founders, based on Psalm 68:11,
"The Lord gave the word and great was the company of those who published it."

Book design copyright © 2009 by Tate Publishing, LLC. All rights reserved.
Cover design by Leah LeFlore
Interior design by Stefanie Rooney

Published in the United States of America

ISBN: 978-1-60696-068-4
1. Biography & Autobiography, Medical
2. Religion, Christian Life, Inspirational
09.01.06

Acknowledgments

I am grateful to many people who have had an influence on my life and on this project.

There is not enough paper and ink to list them all, but a few deserve special mention.

A special thank you to my beautiful wife, Sharon, who has been a shining light in my life since the day I first met her. Her love, support, and belief have always been with me. I am the first to admit that I married "up."

To Sharon's sister and my friend, Ann Moore, who worked tirelessly with me to ensure that Sharon received the best care during her illness and who "kept me off of the ledge" during a very trying period, I say a big thank you. I could not have done it alone.

Thank you to my father and mother, Jack and Carolyn Hanlon, for the countless sacrifices they have made over the years. It is only as I have gotten older that I fully realize the magnitude of those sacrifices and understand a love that has no bounds.

Thank you to all of my brothers and sisters: Maryanne, Carol, Jack, Patricia, Katherine, Anne Marie, Dan, and Chris, who are all a bunch of "good eggs," although I think that a few may be slightly cracked. Yeah, I know, it takes one to know one! They have made life fun and adventurous and are always around no matter what.

And last, but not least, special thanks to God, our heavenly Father, for the countless blessings and strength Sharon and I have received.

Table of Contents

Foreword

Time—do we ever have as much as we need to do everything that we view as important, or even sometimes vital, to the quality and success of our lives? We try to control it and make it stretch, certain that we can do one more thing before we finally rest for the day. There are obvious things that slow us down momentarily, and then there are also those insidious events that hit us with such impact that they can leave us reeling in their wake. It is at these moments that we learn some crucial things about ourselves and the people we cherish the most.

For a period of five months, my husband, Bob, served as my voice during a time of extreme adversity, as I lay motionless from paralysis and clung to life while a ventilator took my every breath. The demon trying to take me from Bob, my sons, family, and friends was Guillain-Barré Syndrome. It is one of those illnesses that we learn about through personal experience, as it is not a topic usually discussed during idle conversation.

In *The Twist in the Road*, Bob will take you on a journey that has spanned almost two decades. You will be amazed as he guides you through a course of events that began with his near-fatal airplane accident. Along this journey, he offers insight about our bodies and our minds, as well as the health-care system, as he shares some stories that will make you laugh and realize the value of humor in some of the least humorous situations, all while emphasizing the tenacity of the human spirit, especially when guided by faith.

His love and commitment have no bounds, and I took great solace knowing that he was watching over me. I would listen closely for his distinctive footsteps, his hearty laugh, and his upbeat conversation with the medical staff as he arrived at the hospital each day. He would always greet me with, "Hello, beautiful," and although mirrors were kept far from my view, I often wondered if we'd need to make an eye exam for him our first priority once this ordeal was over. I knew that I could rely on his knowledgeable and insistent nature so everything would be handled properly. He was determined that no more danger would befall me *on his watch*. We still had a lot of living and loving to do together.

Bob and I have what we refer to as the "Eleventh Commandment," which states, "Thou shalt not fool thyself." The stakes were high, and, realizing that a successful outcome would not be the result of a solo act, Bob quickly enlisted my sister, Ann, as a partner in what would be a battle of strength, exhaustion, belief, and fear. What a ride we all took during those months. For me, Ann was a lifeline to my sons and our family but, most of all, a source of peacefulness. In those early and most frightening weeks, she would leave each night by stroking my hair and quietly saying, "Every day, every step of the way, I'll be right here."

All of the visits and cards from family and friends were an important part of the equation during my recovery; however, as every mother knows, your children, whether youngsters or young adults, are always on your mind. I am grateful that my sons, Dan and Rob, were young adults during my illness. My spirits would always lift with the sight of them, and I would smile inside at their constant greetings of "Hi, Mom, you look great today, better all the time," happy that they were keeping a positive attitude.

Sometimes our best effort, or at least what we *believe* to be our best effort, just isn't enough. It is during these times that we have no choice but to dig deeper, far deeper into our heart and soul, and then go all the way. It is during these times that we find just what it is that we are truly prepared to do in order to win. To triumph over this illness, I knew I would have to draw on all of my inner strength, which was supported by my belief that God was watching over me, although I must admit that I did ask for any extra guardian angels that might be available. I have always been fortunate that in times of strife I can settle my fears and find my inner sanctuary through prayer and a mental trip to the ocean. Whether the scene is a calm and serene ocean or waves crashing along the jetty, add some warm sunshine, and I become focused on the possibilities, determined to beat the enemy.

My unyielding determination to win was fueled by several things. First was my intense love for Bob, our future, and the people who needed us. Second, I wanted my sons to see and understand that no matter how difficult we may find a situation to be, we keep fighting. Giving up was not an option, as the thought of leaving them was unbearable. And third, my two brothers, two sisters, and I lost both of our parents too early in life, and I was going to fight as hard as I could not to put them through another loss. There was still a lot of laughter in our future.

Much of what we face in life can be summed up in a story of inspiration which I want to pass on to you before I invite you to share our journey as Bob has written it with such care, love, and laughter. The story is about a farmer who had a beloved mule, and one day the mule fell into a deep well on the man's property. He heard fearful braying from the mule and went to find him so deep in the well that he wasn't sure if he could rescue him. He summoned help from his neighbors, and using ropes and other devices, they tried unsuccessfully to lift the mule to safety. Unable to bear the fearful braying of his mule, the farmer felt the only humane thing to do was bury him alive, and so he and his friends began to throw dirt down the well. The mule was even more terrified, and as each shovelful of dirt hit his back, he would simply shake it off and step on it. The mule continued to shake off all of the dirt that landed on him and would step up as the dirt filled the well.

Soon, enough dirt had been thrown down, and the mule had shaken it off until he had risen to the top of the well and stepped out to safety. The moral of the story is that even in the most desperate of situations, the answer is as simple as *shake it off and step up to the fight. Never quit!*

Sharon

Introduction

One day Sharon said to me, "I feel as though I was driving along, suddenly there was a twist in the road, and I ran smack into a tree." She was referring to the sudden onset of a disease that almost claimed her life.

As we go through life, there are often twists and turns and bumps in the road. My father used to refer to these events as "life throwing us a curve ball." Pop had a way with words and was always a great teacher, especially in areas of common sense and values. He constantly challenged me and my siblings to think. He always said that it was his responsibility to make sure that we had "the right tools in our toolbox" when we went out into the world on our own. Of course he was not referring to physical tools, such as hammers or wrenches, but those that make us mentally prepared to face the issues of everyday life.

As time went on, I came to realize just how much I would have to rely on the foundation that he laid so many years ago. The twists, turns, and bumps that I refer to are the unexpected problems we face in life, so many of which are out of our control. It has often been said that the measure of a man or woman is how they react to a problem.

In 1990, I was involved in a serious airplane accident, which left me with paralysis below the waist. Following several surgeries and months of hospitalization and rehabilitation, I spent the next several years attempting to rebuild my life. I was determined to walk again and often faced negative attitudes from others who did not believe that it was possible. Using leg braces, crutches, and sheer determination, I managed to make that dream into reality. The worst was behind me.

I then met the most wonderful lady in the world. Sharon is absolutely beautiful, and she captured my heart immediately. We married in 1996 and quickly settled into life as newlyweds. I won't go so far as to say that I took her for granted; however, in my own naïve way, I just assumed that we would live happily ever after and life would go on as usual. She had experienced a few health issues; however, they were manageable. And so, life went on.

That was until Sharon came to the twist in the road. In 2006 Sharon became gravely ill with Guillain-Barré Syndrome. In the span of only twenty-four short hours, she was transformed from a vivacious active lady to being totally paralyzed and on life support. She was now going to be facing physical and mental struggles as I had years ago, only worse. A ventilator machine was breathing for her, and she was fighting not only for her every breath, but also for her life.

I had often teased Sharon and said that "her momma grew her strong." I was about to learn in the coming months just exactly how true that was. And her father had taught her how to always look at the lighter side of things. Although Frank and Helen are in Heaven, there was no doubt that they were pulling for her as she struggled during this horrific ordeal.

The fact is that things happen to all of us every day. Sometimes we must work very hard, both physically and mentally, to overcome problems and obstacles that we are faced with. When my brother Jack and I played football at Archmere Academy, the coaches always stressed upon us that winning was 99% *inspiration* and 1% *perspiration*. Yes, I realize that Thomas Edison once referred to those statistics in reverse order. He was talking about *genius;* however, I'm talking about *winning!* I'm talking about keeping our heads in the game and surviving.

Therefore, I submit to you that overcoming the issues that we face in life is more about attitude than anything else. I realize it is true that education, intelligence, or skill can help us solve a problem, and that even money can buy us options at times. But I truly believe that nothing can ever take the place of, or carry us further than, a positive attitude.

We have also found that a sense of humor can go a long way, and I've included some of our lighter moments in this story as well. We have had no choice but to laugh at a lot of things along the way. Life is too short. So by all means, take some time in life now and then to stop for a moment and laugh a little. Heck, laugh a lot until it hurts. It works for us.

I am about to take you on a little journey, one that has lasted for many years and is still ongoing. While the major obstacles we both faced were of a medical nature, we have certainly had many experiences in life and have learned from them. Many of the lessons we have learned and the principles by which we have lived can really be applied to any part of life. Situations and methods of doing things may vary; however, principles don't. The lessons we have learned are invaluable, and we have been blessed to have had many wonderful people touch our lives.

Despite the obstacles we have faced, much has been given to us, most of all, God's love and blessings. I was once told that to whom much is given, much is expected. It is that statement that has compelled me to write this book and share with you some of the gifts that we have received and lessons that we have learned on our journey.

Throughout the story, I have changed a few names to protect the privacy of some, and I figured that it wouldn't hurt too much to keep just a few of 'em guessing. But then again, a lot of this story wasn't exactly low profile in this neck of the woods. So everyone pretty much knows who the players are if they know of or were part of the story. Anyway, relax, kick back, and read on. I hope you enjoy.

Bob

The Accident

When I turned the key, I saw the propeller blades become a blur as the engine sprang to life. The smell of exhaust from one-hundred-octane fuel was a familiar and welcome intrusion through the open door into the cockpit. As I taxied to the runway, my mind was focused on the pending flight as well as the events planned for that afternoon. There was one other thing on my mind—I kept hearing my mother's voice. I had briefly visited her that morning, and while Mom was not apprehensive about flying in general, she had expressed concern that day. For some reason, Mom felt uneasy and had asked me not to fly. Call it intuition. I had assured her that there was nothing to worry about, and besides, I was a grown man. I was certainly old enough to make my own decisions. But it doesn't matter how old any of us get. The fact remains, our mother will always worry about us and try to protect us from any harm.

I finished performing all of the necessary pre-takeoff checks, closed and latched the door, and taxied onto the runway. After one last visual scan of the instruments, I smoothly pushed the throttle lever forward and released the brakes. As the airplane gained momentum, my visual scan alternated between the runway and the instrument panel. When I reached takeoff speed, I pulled back on the control wheel to raise the nose and felt the wheels leave the runway. I smiled, just as I had every time that I had taken off in the past. Once again I was flying, and there isn't much that can compare to the feeling of defying gravity and leaving the earth behind.

As I gained altitude, I departed the area and turned on course toward my destination. It was an overcast day, but nice nonetheless with little wind, and I was glad that the weather had cooperated. Before long, I was over my landing site, and my life was about to be changed forever.

When I began my day on September 9, 1990, I truly believed that it would be just another day. I was looking forward to making use of the license I had worked so hard to earn and in the process share the fun of aviation with some friends. I was working as a mechanic for a car dealership at the time, and I was to fly to a company picnic at a coworker's farm in Lancaster County, Pennsylvania. He had a large parcel of land, and many were looking forward to my bringing the airplane and taking people for rides. At least that *was* the plan.

I had previously been out to the farm and walked the field where I was to land. It was promising to be a great day. Unfortunately, the plane that I had reserved for rental was a model that I would later learn had some nasty stalling tendencies as a result of some design issues, earning it the most unflattering of nicknames, the *Traumahawk*. This information only came to light years later, after a series of investigations and flight tests following a string of similar accidents. However, it was kind of a moot point for me, as I was about to learn the hard way. I was also about to learn another lesson—one should *always* listen to their mother!

I had flown that airplane before, yet that day something about it just felt different. As I was preparing to land, I decided to abort the mission and take the plane back to the airport. I simply wasn't comfortable with the way the airplane was performing. I pushed the throttle forward and raised the nose of the plane, and as I was climbing out, the airplane stalled. The last thing I remembered was seeing the ground rushing up at me. Yeah, I know, I was falling and the ground wasn't really rising, but it sure looked that way.

The next thing I knew, I was sitting in a mangled airplane in a field, knowing full well that my back was broken. I was bleeding from somewhere but was not sure of the full extent of my injuries. I cannot even begin to describe the flood of thoughts and emotions running through my mind at that instant. My thoughts ranged from, *Well, this didn't turn out too well,* all the way to, *Is this thing going to catch fire and blow up?* and everything in between. Plus, I had managed to pull this off in front of a large crowd of people. Way to go. There's nothing like looking stupid and having an audience.

I was not able to get out of the plane, as my seat had broken and slammed forward, planting my face against the instrument panel. That explained the bleeding. And there was that small issue of my back being broken. I wasn't going anywhere in a hurry, and although I desperately wanted to get out of the plane, I knew that I had to wait until my spine was immobilized.

I would later find out that my spine was actually fractured in three areas. The twelfth thoracic (T12) vertebrae had burst, and the fourth and fifth lumbar (L4-L5) vertebrae had also been compromised. This was not turning out to be a very good day. Fortunately, I was the only person on board. I remember at the time thinking how great it was that I could still move my legs. At least I wasn't paralyzed. Unfortunately, my excitement was a little premature, and by the time I was extricated from the plane and being transported, I had lost sensation and mobility in both of my legs.

The pain in my back was excruciating, almost as if it were on fire. Fortunately, the paramedics had some wonderful drugs on board the ambulance that went a long way toward dealing with the pain. Also, I was in shock but conscious and aware of what was going on. But it was almost as if I were in another place. This was a first for me.

I recall from my days as an Emergency Medical Technician (EMT) seeing similar situations as I treated accident victims; however, I had never seen this side of it. In class we were taught the textbook definition of shock, but now I was getting the real lesson. I believe that shock is God's way of putting you in another place temporarily to keep you from going out of your mind. I truly do. The morphine did help a little too. Okay, it helped a lot!

It was a lengthy ride in the ambulance, and at some point on the trip, the morphine was running low. The other paramedic vehicle was following the ambulance, so they pulled over to the side of the road so one of the crew could run back and get more from the other vehicle. I remember the one paramedic yelling to the one with me, saying, "How much morphine do you need?" I also remember that *I* yelled back, "How much do they have back there? Bring it all!" I pretty much would have tried anything at that point to kill the pain.

The additional morphine caused things to get a little fuzzy; however, I recall arriving at the emergency room and talking with the staff there. I was extremely upset that I was in this situation and really didn't want to talk about what happened. I was embarrassed, but most of all, I was angry with myself. I had put myself in a situation that I shouldn't have. They asked me if I was allergic to anything, and the only answer I could think of was, "Yeah, gravity seems to be a real problem these days!"

It was mid-afternoon by that point. The staff had asked me if there was anybody that they should call, and I told them no. Actually, all of my family was at Mom and Pop's house for a gathering, and I had planned on stopping by there later after the company picnic. What was going through my mind was that if someone called my family, it would really spoil the gathering.

All right, I'll admit that was pretty silly, but I wasn't thinking very clearly by that point. Intense pain and morphine have a way of clouding one's judgment. Between my reclusive demeanor and my not wanting them to call anyone, they came to an erroneous conclusion and asked me if I had crashed on purpose. I couldn't believe that they were serious. I assured them that if that had been my intention, I would have picked an altitude much higher than a hundred feet or so. And that was about it. I was not aware of any further conversation, as I was pretty heavily sedated by that point.

It is often said that it pays to be in the right place at the right time. There was a practice, which I was told was relatively new at the time, of administering steroid-based drugs to patients with spinal cord injuries, as it was found to be very effective in reducing swelling in the spinal column, thereby limiting paralysis. The one catch is that it must be administered quickly. Fortunately, I was still within the allowable time window for it to be effective, and the doctor treating me was familiar with this practice. I was taken to surgery where Harrington rods (metal rods) were installed in my back to support the area around the T12 vertebrae.

At some point throughout all of that time, I must have been talking about my family, as someone had pinned a note to me that read, "His parents are alive and live in Concordville, Pennsylvania." That was really all of the information they had on me, as I was single, had recently moved, and had not yet updated the address on my license.

From surgery I was taken to the intensive care unit, where I was closely monitored. By that point it was past midnight, and someone from the hospital had found my parents' phone number. None of us ever have a good feeling when the phone rings in the middle of the night. A late-night call coupled with a mother's intuition, Mom knew what was coming.

When it comes to their children, mothers know everything. God had a plan when it came to mothers, and it was a good one. Nobody knows us better or will stand by us like our mother. I was expected to be visiting for dinner and never showed. That's not my style, and Mom was well aware of that. Aware that I was flying, and having tried desperately to talk me out of it, Mom had actually stayed up to watch the late news to see if there had been any accidents. It is almost as if she was expecting the call.

My oldest sister, Maryanne, a registered nurse, had been working the night shift for years in the emergency room at one of our local hospitals. As I mentioned earlier, timing is everything. It just so happened that on this particular night, they were overstaffed, so leaving work was not a problem.

When she got the call from Mom, I would bet

the phone wasn't even hung up yet and the wheels on her car were turning. Maryanne met Mom and Pop *en route* and continued the ride out to Lancaster to view the bad news firsthand. I am told that I didn't look all that good, to say the least. Mom later told me that even Maryanne, despite her nursing experience, had a difficult time with what she saw. The pain that they felt seeing a loved one hanging on to life was not something I could even imagine. That was something I was going to have to wait sixteen years to experience.

Mom, Pop, and Maryanne met with the attending physician and reviewed my case. It's always a plus to have someone in the family with medical training to decipher everything that is being said. It quickly became evident that I would be better off in Philadelphia at Thomas Jefferson University Hospital. The locals refer to it as "Jeff."

Interestingly enough, the attending doctor had trained at Jefferson and was in full agreement. Pop dialed the phone and woke up my uncle, Edward McLaughlin. Uncle Edward was a well-renowned surgeon, and anybody who was anybody in the Philadelphia surgical community knew him well. Fortunately, he had been a lifelong associate of one of the top orthopedic surgeons at Jefferson. The wheels had been put into motion.

My Trip to the Big City

It was September 10, the day after my accident, and I was going to be transferred from Lancaster to Philadelphia. The last thing on my mind at the time would have been anything involving flying, but I was being packed up for a helicopter flight. I can honestly say that I really didn't have any feelings one way or the other. And it's not as if I had a choice. I was somewhat aware of what was going to be taking place; however, I was sedated enough to not really care.

All I really cared about was that I had been given a little button that I could push to self-administer morphine to my IV line as needed for pain. Life couldn't get any better at that point! I do recall one member of the flight team explaining to me how the morphine dispenser worked. He said, "It's sort of like autopilot." All I recall saying was, "Hey, no pilot jokes!" I guess I was still a little sensitive about the whole crashing thing. It wasn't long after the helicopter landed at Jeff that I was headed for the operating room. I was in the hands of the best. The surgical team removed one of my ribs and part of my hip in order to have bone to fuse my spine. I ended up with quite a collection of parts and hardware in my back. Yes, I still set off metal detectors.

My next recollection was being in the neurosensory intensive care unit (NICU) on the ninth floor. For the first time since the accident, I was fully aware of my surroundings and aware that some family members were present. And it was at this point that although heavily sedated, I came to realize the gravity of my situation. I was not able to move anything below my waist. I cried.

While I realized that it was too soon to tell what the outcome would be, what I knew intellectually and what I felt emotionally were vastly different. Sometimes we do have more to fear than fear itself. The prospect of not walking again was overwhelming. My faith was being tested immensely, and while I prayed to God for strength and courage, I will admit that a part of me was playing the "why me?" game.

My thoughts were racing in a thousand directions. There I was, twenty-nine years old, paralyzed from the waist down. I still had a lifetime ahead of me and had no idea what was in my future. I had visions of spending my life in a wheelchair or being permanently bedridden. Or maybe I would recover after all; I just didn't know. Neither did anybody else at that point. My thoughts would go from fear to anger to embarrassment, and then I would be angry with myself for letting my emotions get the best of me.

I would think about all of the things I used to do effortlessly and wonder if I would ever be able to do them again. What would happen if I didn't recover? Would I be able to take care of myself? Would I ever find someone that would love me in this condition, or would I spend the rest of my life alone?

I was having a difficult time adjusting to all of this and even more so adjusting to having total strangers take care of all of my needs, some of which were very personal.

There was one particular nurse who was like an angel to me. One night I was having a particularly hard time dealing with all that was happening. Jamie had finished her shift at eleven p.m. but stayed around for a few hours to talk with me.

From the first time I met Jamie, I could tell that she was truly a caring person, so it really came as no surprise when she reached out to me. While I had never voiced any of my concerns, I am quite certain that my struggles were obvious. Jamie put my mind at ease and did more that night than she will ever know. She had just finished a long day and had a husband to go home to. She didn't need to do what she did; however, I was grateful that God had sent her to me.

I didn't get the chance to say good-bye to Jamie; however, I made a point of going back months later to give her a hug and thank her. It was the start of a great new thing for me.

I was never a big "hugger" prior to my accident, but now I'm okay with it. There aren't too many things in this world that can beat a good hug. I learned one other thing that day—that such a visit can mean more to the recipient than it did to me. Those that work with trauma patients rarely get to see the fruits of their labor. More often than not, the patient moves to a step-down unit or to rehab, and they don't get to see the outcome. It really does their heart good to see one of their patients up and about.

––––––––––––––

My family, along with a few friends, continued to visit constantly to support me and keep my spirits up, sometimes too much. One evening I had to have two of my brothers thrown out. One of my incisions ran from my chest all the way around to the center of my back and had been stapled closed. Jack and Chris were carrying on so much and had me laughing so hard that I was in severe pain and had visions of staples blowing out. I had to have the nurse ask them to leave. But, what the heck, if your brothers can't torment you a little bit now and then, what good are they? Somehow I believe that if we were all a real serious bunch, I never would have made it through this. A sense of humor goes a long way; however, it just hurt too much to laugh any more at that point. As a result of being intubated several times, which is where an airway tube is placed down your throat, I was very uncomfortable and had become the poster child for sore throat remedies. So naturally, every visitor with good intentions brought me a bag of cough drops. I probably had a year's supply at one point.

The first time I tried to eat food, it happened to be breakfast. I'm not sure what anybody was thinking, but they brought me corn flakes. Now don't get me wrong, I've always liked corn flakes. But there I was, paralyzed, flat on my back, not allowed to sit up because my back was unstable, and I was trying to eat corn flakes. I'm sure you can envision the challenge of trying to get a spoonful of cereal with milk from a bedside tray to one's mouth without wearing it. Needless to say, the bedding needed freshening, and I now understood why I was going to be losing weight!

After several days I was told that I was going to be put in a cast to keep me immobile.

The good news just kept on coming. As if I didn't have enough on my mind, I was going to be wrapped up in plaster for the next three months. Great—just great! I was doing my best to avoid sinking into a deep depression, and it was not easy. For the first time, I began to question if I would not have been better off if I had died in the accident. I had a few days to lament about all of this, as they needed to wait for my incisions to heal enough to remove the staples prior to casting. That was a real treat, having several dozen staples pulled out of my skin.

I was put in a body cast that went from the top of my chest down to my knee and quickly learned the true meaning of what it meant to be immobile. The technician in the cast room was a man named Tony. He was one of the funniest persons I had ever met. His quick wit and caring approach made the process go smoothly, and he was finished before I knew it.

At the time, casting materials were available in colors, and with Halloween just around the corner, I chose orange. I'll admit that it was a pretty lame choice, so I'm just going to chalk it up to the influence of the medications I was on. One of my sisters took a black marker and drew eyes and a mouth on it to make me look like a jack-o-lantern. I was the talk of the town. One of these days, I'll get even with her for that!

The cast was so tight around me that I could barely breathe. Of course they had to make the cast that tight in preparation for the weight that I would lose, which ultimately ended up being roughly forty pounds. Oftentimes folks ask what it was like to be in that cast and be immobile for such a long time. Probably the best description I can give is to jack up a car, crawl under it, and then have a friend (or an enemy) lower the car down—and not come back for three months! In addition to not being able to breathe, I couldn't go anywhere; if something itched I couldn't scratch it, and eating was quite a challenge since I was horizontal all of the time. I remember begging the nurses to put oxygen on me, as I was convinced I was going to die from asphyxia. Looking back, probably all it did was make me believe that I was breathing easier. However, I was content for the time being.

I kept on praying for strength and courage, and finally I began to view this situation as temporary. Now that I was stable and had my body cast on, I was moved down to the third floor to the spinal cord rehab wing—a place that I would call home for a while. It had been almost two weeks since my accident and would be the first time that I would have interaction with any other patients. Initially, I wasn't looking forward to it, as a small part of me was still busy having a little pity party. Well, actually, I was having a big pity party.

One day that all changed. I saw a young man that was half of my age who was a quadriplegic. He was wearing a halo, which was screwed into his skull, and he was propelling his wheelchair by blowing into a tube. He couldn't move his hands, arms, or legs, and I had heard that his prognosis was not good. This was my epiphany—an instant attitude adjustment. At that moment I made the decision that I was not going to allow self-pity to ever get the best of me. I was stronger than that.

Fighting wasn't optional anymore; it was mandatory. I had to continue to move forward. I had to stop doubting myself, but most of all, I couldn't allow myself to doubt God. Between God and my family, I had a winning team behind me. I just had to maintain my belief.

Not to mention that I was in the best hospital in the area. I had access to the best resources and the best people. The doctors were first class and were always encouraging.

Almost immediately after getting to that ward, they handed me a large book to read and study. These people weren't just about patient care but also about education.

When a person suffers a significant neurological disorder such as a spinal cord injury, their life is often altered permanently. It was important, as the patient, to learn as much as possible about all of these changes.

While all of the information in the handbook didn't apply to every patient, it was rather unsettling to read about what *might* lie in the future for me. Some patients suffer neurological disorders or injuries and make complete recoveries. Others are not so fortunate. The list of complications can be quite long depending on the level of the injury, complications that go well beyond whether a person will walk again.

Issues often cover a broad range, such as respiratory problems, bowel and bladder complications, and infections, as well as blood clots and skin problems from being sedentary. Some of the issues I could call my own; others I avoided. Heparin shots were a daily event to prevent blood clots. Prior to being put into the cast, they would administer the shots in my belly. Once I had been put in my cast, they would inject them into my right thigh, which had been left exposed. Either way, it was not my favorite activity. Imagine lighting a match and holding it against your skin—it feels that good.

I marveled at not only the professionalism of the doctors but also at their compassion. They gave a new meaning to the term "bedside manner." I always had a list of questions and issues, and they never rushed or acted as if they didn't have time to address them. One of the team in particular was my favorite. Dr. Graziani was a very kind and sweet lady and not too hard to look at, if I may say so. Needless to say, I looked forward to rounds every morning.

I was in a rather large room with three room-mates, one of whom was a particularly funny fellow. We called him Pedro, as we did not know his real name. He had been shot during an "entrepreneurial venture," so to speak, and was registered as a John Doe so that hopefully none of the other business associates could find him and finish the job. He claimed that he spoke no English, yet he miraculously seemed to understand everything we said. The Spanish classes I took in high school paid off, though. We got along great and shared many laughs, but a little part of me always wondered if his associates (or enemies) would ever find him or, even worse, shoot at the wrong bed. One particular scenario kept playing in my mind. I envisioned a few shady characters coming into the room in the middle of the night and saying, "Was he in 368C or 368D? Never mind—hit 'em both!" I was in D. As a result of that uneasy feeling, I always slept with one eye open, just in case I had to hit the floor!

Being in a room with three other patients, pri-vacy was not a common thing. I have always been a private person; well, I was up until that point. Even though there were curtains that could be drawn, the constant traffic in and out of the patient areas made them a moot point. At first, I was a little taken back by all of it but quickly came to the conclusion that modesty is only for wimps.

Even though my body was in the cast, not *all* of it was covered. If I was uncovered for some reason and someone needed the nurse who was with me, they just pulled the curtain and walked in. This is not in the form of a complaint; it is simply a fact. Privacy only exists in a private room, and that wasn't happening on the rehab floor.

One of the patients in my room was an older man, and his fifty-something daughter used to come in every morning to help him get dressed and ready for the day. So there I was, getting a sponge bath on the few parts of me that were exposed, and she pulled the curtain, stuck her head in, and said, "Good morning, Bob!" The first thought in my head was, *Lady, can't you see I'm not dressed?* However, I simply smiled and replied, "Good morning." From that point on, every morning she would walk right in to say hello and ask if I needed anything.

I got over being shy very quickly. While I had been startled at first, I really wasn't offended at all. I figured that I probably have all of the typical parts everyone else has, and if I have something nobody has ever seen before, hopefully they'd let me know so I can get into the Guinness record book.

The nurses did their best, but they were doing a high-volume business, and a curtain can only do so much. I think everyone just got used to it, so much so that I think it was several months after I went home before I stopped feeling strange bathing without an audience. It just wasn't the same! Activities which had at one point in my life been private had become a spectator sport.

To this day, I have a special place in my heart for nurses, especially those that work in the rehab field. They are a tough crew. They have to do most, if not all of the things that patients need to do, as the patients can't do it for themselves. They work hard, with much of their work being very physical. Most of the patients, myself included, couldn't even get out of bed on their own and into a wheelchair. Their job is not an easy one. But most of all, they had such a caring approach to their work. I hope there is a special place in Heaven for all of them.

The nurses were real sticklers when it came to skin care. Decubitis ulcers, also known as bed sores, are a real threat to patients who remain sedentary. They are caused by pressure on certain areas of the body and blood flow being restricted to the skin if the patient stays in that position too long. Basically, the skin dies. The problem is exacerbated when a person is paralyzed, as they often lack sensation.

If the average person sits in one position too long, parts of their body often get numb or "fall asleep," as the saying goes. That is our body's way of telling us that we need to move. A person lacking sensation no longer has that advantage. We must remember to move around—to change positions and shift our weight.

It is my belief that there is absolutely no reason for a healthy person to ever have any skin breakdown.

This medical team was of the same philosophy, and they were not going to let it happen on their watch. They were extremely vigilant about turning patients in bed so they didn't lie in one position too long, as well as doing weight shifts when patients were in wheelchairs. They used to flip us over backwards in our wheelchairs and leave us in that position for fifteen minutes or so to take the weight off of our butts so we didn't get skin problems there either.

The nurses also stressed that it was *our* responsibility as the patient to remember to shift. After all, they were not going to be coming home with us, and for many patients like myself, this would be a lifetime issue. So we had to get used to taking care of ourselves.

————————

As I became more comfortable with my surroundings, I couldn't help but start getting to know other patients and learn of how they came to be there. Some of the stories were truly amazing, others heartbreaking, and many patients admitted that it was their own foolishness that brought them to their demise. If I had a dime for every person who became injured due to diving into shallow water, I'd be a rich man.

One woman was a real-life example of the saying "No good deed goes unpunished." She had fallen while trying to get a cat out of a tree for a child in her neighborhood. She had broken both of her legs in addition to her back. So she had a cast similar to mine but more restrictive, and hers was a pretty shade of pink. Her attitude was remarkably good given her situation and that which led to it. I don't remember her name; however, I enjoyed talking with her whenever I could, as I found her to be inspiring and encouraging. Whenever I encountered patients that were in worse shape than I was but who were able to maintain a good attitude, I was able to take the focus off of myself. And I figured that if they could do it, then I could do it. My heart truly went out to all of these people. Hindsight is a wonderful thing, but I guess mostly we just don't believe that something grave is going to happen to us. One man from New Jersey had been in an explosion on an industrial site. He was a quadriplegic and on a ventilator. Keith and his wife were absolutely the nicest people you could ever meet. We ended up going through rehab together and sort of ended up being each other's support team. I mean, here was a guy who not only knocked at death's door but had momentarily crossed the threshold. If he ever felt sorry for himself, it never showed, and it never interfered with his ability to be one of my biggest cheerleaders.

All in all, we were mostly a group of people who had been in the wrong place at the wrong time on the wrong day and had ended up at the same place in order to deal with whatever was wrong with each of us. Sometimes I felt as if we were just a big group of misfits. Every time I turned a corner, I met another person with another horrific story. So much pain and suffering everywhere, and all of us were a captive audience as well as participants.

My family continued to support me, both mentally and spiritually. My sister Maryanne, given her nursing background, remained actively involved in any medical issues. I learned very early on the importance of patient advocacy. There is so much to know and learn when going through an event like this, and I was fortunate to have a good team behind me. When I look around in this world at people that have accomplished great things, few have done it alone. I believe that teamwork is essential to obtaining good results and that we all need the support of others. Most of all, we need God's love and blessing. However, I must admit that, at times, it seemed as though I was never going to see a light at the end of the tunnel, let alone reach the end.

One day my sister Patricia brought me a Saint Jude medal and a card with a short verse on it called "Don't Quit." It reads as follows:

Don't Quit
When things go wrong as they sometimes will,
When the road you're trudging seems all uphill,
When the funds are low and the debts are high,
And you want to smile, but you have to sigh,
When care is pressing you down a bit,
Rest, if you must, but don't you quit.
Life is queer with its twists and turns,
As every one of us sometimes learns,
And many a failure turns about,
When he might have won had he stuck it out;

Don't give up though the pace seems slow—
You may succeed with another blow.
Success is failure turned inside out,
The silver tint of the clouds of doubt,
And you never can tell how close you are,
It may be near when it seems so far;
So stick to the fight when you're hardest hit—
It's when things seem worst that you must not quit.

While the verse seemed so simplistic, the messages that I received were very powerful. The fact that Patricia gave it to me told me that she believed I would triumph in the end. And the more I read the verse, the more I was reminded that we are often closer to reaching our goals than we realize. We just need to get back up every time we fall.

Almost two decades later, it is showing its age, but I still carry that card and the medal on me every day. Those words kept me from quitting then and still inspire me today. And so, since quitting was not an option, every day I would wheel myself down to the physical therapy room and exercise what little of my body wasn't restricted by the cast.

If someone were to ask me what the hospital looked like, I probably would have described the ceiling. Being flat on my back in a body cast, I had a very limited view of things. My total world consisted of my room, the hallway, and the therapy gym, and most of it I saw from a horizontal position. People would call me about coming to visit and ask how to find my room. I was clueless. I had arrived by helicopter and come in through the roof, so they were on their own.

And somehow they all did manage to find me. I had many visitors, some which I hardly knew. Once in a while it made for an interesting situation. Nobody likes a situation when they can't remember someone's name. One day my father was visiting me, and one of my brother Jack's friends stopped in to see me. Now, it's important to understand two things. Pop is a fairly straight-laced guy, and this gal, who could definitely hold her own in the looks department, was dressed in a way that left little to the imagination.

I had only been introduced to her once and couldn't remember her name. She came bopping into the room with balloons, a magazine, and an ice cream cone for me. "Oh boy," I muttered under my breath. "How do I explain this?"

No problem, I thought, *I'll just introduce my father, and then, naturally, she'll say who she is.* So I said to her, "Hi, nice to see you. This is my father, Jack Hanlon." (He and my brother share the same name.) All she could muster up was a "hello." I was really hoping she would have taken the cue and said what her name was. *Great*, I thought, *my brother certainly isn't dating her for her brains.* Of course that was already obvious just by looking at her. All I could tell Pop was that she was one of my brother's friends. This happened again a few days later with another one of his girlfriends, and yes, you guessed it—Pop was there at the time. I offered the same explanation that the second gal was another of Jack's friends. Of course, Jack threw me under the bus and denied all of it.

In fact, to this day, he still denies knowing these girls, leaving my father to believe that all of my younger days were misspent on floozies. Not that I minded the visits, though.

Being confined in the hospital was taking its toll on me, so I was happy to see anybody.

Finally one day I got someone to take me downstairs and roll me outside. After weeks of being indoors, the sunshine felt wonderful. There I was, flat out in a body cast on a reclined wheelchair on the sidewalk of Eleventh Street in Philadelphia. I welcomed even the diesel exhaust from the buses. I was outside. I could look up at the sky. I could hear the sounds of people going about their everyday business. I just wanted to get out of that cast and try to walk; however, that was going to have to wait until December. Unfortunately, it was only late September, and I was already losing my patience with trying to be patient!

In physical therapy I was pretty much limited to working on upper-body strength. That was going to be crucial, as I would spend time in the foreseeable future using a wheelchair. I remember the first time they tried to stand me vertical. I lasted eight seconds and got light-headed, and that was it. I needed to get stronger.

Looking back, I believe that one of my motivations to get better was my occupational therapist (OT). In occupational therapy, they deal with helping you learn how to perform all of the tasks necessary in everyday life, such as bathing, getting dressed, grooming, and cooking, all of what are known as *activities of daily living,* or ADLs (OT jargon) for short.

Oftentimes when people have physical limitations, they must use adaptive equipment to assist themselves in performing certain tasks. I called them gadgets and wanted no part of them. I'm only slightly hardheaded and saw this as a choice to either get better or use those blasted gadgets. She was insistent that I was going to learn how to pull pants on over the body cast using some of the "adaptive equipment." (Remember, I couldn't bend and reach my feet.) I saw no point to it since I wasn't going to be in the cast for the rest of my life. Every morning one of the nurses would put a pair of scrubs on me so I was covered. So why did I need to do this? It's not as if I was going to put on a suit and go to the office while wearing the cast forever. My OT and I didn't always see eye to eye, but we reached a reasonable compromise with some of these issues. We finally agreed that she would stop trying to make me put pants on using gadgets, and I would play nicely and bake cookies with some of the other patients. Needless to say, I make a much better patient advocate than I do a patient.

Looking back now, it was actually pretty funny, but at the time I probably frustrated her to no end. She was a sweet girl, and I realize she had my best interests at heart. I did the best that I could to get stronger but was really going to have to wait until I was out of the body cast to make great strides (pun intended). Once that happened, I would go to a rehabilitation hospital where I could maximize my efforts.

I was grateful for one of the OT gadgets though. It was a long stick with a hook on the end. I had to wear special knee-high boots at night that were connected to a pump that inflated them at preset intervals to compress my legs. The purpose was to promote blood flow to assist in preventing clots. I couldn't feel very much of anything below the waist, but I could feel *them!* And I hated them. I would use the stick to pry the Velcro straps loose to get the boots off, as I couldn't reach them. Of course the nurses would chide me and put them back on me. This went on all night long, every night.

In addition to healing and getting stronger physically, I was getting an education about life, people, and mostly myself. I had never been pushed to the limits like this at any previous point in my life. It was not easy to do even the simplest of daily tasks, but I believe that being pushed mentally was the most difficult.

Those who cared about me often reminded me that God doesn't give us more than we can handle. I had two thoughts on that. The first was that I know they meant well when they said it. My second thought was that some days I truly wished that God didn't have so much confidence in me. I would often pray and ask God if he could just take my word for it that I was tough. No dice.

Did I have to be tested? Obviously so. I was going to need that strength tenfold, possibly more, in years to come. The only way we can grow is to be stretched and taken out of our mental comfort zone. Sometimes we need to be pushed to our limits. However, the good news is that God knows where our limits are. I just had to trust in Him.

Throughout all that was going on, I would often think, and sometimes worry, about my job and finances. I was not even sure if I would be able to work as a mechanic any longer and, even if I could, if my job would still be open when and if the time came. In addition, I had thousands and thousands of dollars worth of tools at the dealership. Most folks think that those big red toolboxes that mechanics have are supplied by the shop. Not so. We buy them as well as all of the tools that are in them.

But I kept telling myself that I was worrying for nothing. I had worked there for a number of years, and, after all, these people were my friends. Many of them had been to visit me. I needed to concentrate on getting stronger. Since the event on the day of my accident had been company sponsored, I had filed a workman compensation claim, so at least short-term finances didn't have to be a concern. Energy that was being spent worrying was energy that was being wasted. I was certain that my friends weren't going to let me down.

Many have heard the expression "You don't have to go home, but you can't stay here."

Well, after about six weeks, I was told that the time had come for me to leave. This was great news except for a few issues. I was still in the body cast; I couldn't walk and really couldn't do much of anything for myself. And while I needed to go to a physical rehabilitation facility, they wouldn't take a patient in the condition I was in at that point. It was October, and I was scheduled to be in the cast until early December. Well, it was just a small obstacle.

The Waiting Game

Six weeks down, and six more to go in the body cast. I just had to play the waiting game somewhere else. Insurance would have paid for me to go to a nursing home, but I had been through a few nursing homes when I ran fire and ambulance, and the conditions hadn't impressed me. I'm not saying that they are all the same, but the ones I had been through didn't make me feel enthusiastic about that idea. I ended up renting a hospital bed and other necessary equipment and staying with my family.

The night before I left Jefferson Hospital was an interesting one to say the least. The older man who had been across from me was no longer there, and a teenager had taken his place. This boy had part of his leg amputated due to cancer. He was obviously quite popular, because every night brought twenty to thirty teenagers to the room. We emptied every balloon in the room and did what all smart people do with helium. Next thing I knew, I was speaking Spanish to Pedro in a helium-induced high-pitched voice. I never saw him laugh so hard. All he said was "Ay, ay, ay, caramba!" over and over.

Somebody had a copy of *Rolling Stone,* and the young fellow across from me looked just like the punk rocker on the cover, sans the jewelry, makeup, and spiked hair. Well, you can probably imagine that with fifteen to twenty girls visiting him, their purses contained a sufficient amount of cosmetics and hair jazz to do the trick. In a matter of minutes, he was transformed into the person on the magazine cover. Someone even produced a bass guitar like the guy on the magazine cover had—talk about a Kodak moment! Everyone in the room was hysterical.

It was never my style to act silly, but to be truthful, I needed that. It was the first time in quite a while that I had really had a good hearty laugh. I had a lot of pent-up anxiety, fear, and frustration. It felt good to release some of it. Laughter is truly the best medicine, and my body hurt that night from laughing. It was a great hurt.

The noise level caused the nurses to come in and shut down the fun. I didn't sleep very much that night in anticipation of leaving the next day. I was both looking forward to it and nervous at the same time. And I was still sore from laughing so hard.

Morning arrived, and it was hard to say good-bye to everyone. Everyone had been absolutely wonderful, but a few in particular had been especially caring and gracious to me. It is probably difficult for some people to imagine developing such an emotional bond with various staff members. I'm sure that it is equally as difficult for them to not become emotionally attached with patients. I am certain that I would have a very hard time doing the job that they do.

I was no longer active with the fire company, but Mom was. So Mom came downtown with one of the

ambulances, along with one of the other EMTs, Tom
Moore, who was a very funny guy —always the practical joker. It was a sad day when he passed a few
years back. The world could use a few more of him.

Mom and Tom promptly loaded me onto a
stretcher to transport me home. When flying, it
is customary to make sure the area is clear and to
announce you are about to crank the airplane's engine
for the safety of bystanders. So, in keeping with his
comedian-like personality, Tom rolled down the window on the ambulance and yelled, "Clear prop!" out
the window before starting the vehicle. I'll tell you
what, you wreck one little airplane, and everybody is
full of pilot jokes. I would have expected nothing less
from Tom.

We got underway, and before long we arrived at
Mom and Pop's house on Scott Road, which is where
I was to spend the next six weeks. We arrived to find
a state police car there, not a rare occurrence. Over
the years, with all of the family involved with the fire
company, it was not uncommon to find a rescue vehicle or a police car or three at the house while folks
were on coffee break. The house is in the boondocks,
and growing up there was sort of like growing up in
Mayberry. Today, sadly, it is hard to recognize the
area with all of the development that has occurred.
They call it progress, but I'm not too sure.

As I was being rolled through the front door
of the house on a stretcher, I was greeted by Jim,
a trooper who was somewhat new at the time. The
first words out of Tom's mouth were, "Got any bul-

lets in that gun, Barney?" (On *The Andy Griffith Show,* Deputy Barney Fife never had any bullets in his gun.) I guess Jim had never watched any of the old television shows, since he was the only one not doubled over laughing. So we attempted to explain the reference to him. He found a *little* humor in it. All right, make that two people not doubled over. Seeing as I was still in the body cast, I wasn't doing much bending.

I quickly got settled in for what was to be a mentally trying period. In the hospital I had a daily routine that included therapy. Here, I was on my own most of the time. Once or twice a week, a nurse or nurse's aide would stop by and check my condition, and various family members were in and out frequently to check on me. But everyone still had to live their lives, work, and take care of their families, and I fully understood that. So it left me with a lot of solitary time.

While I have never been the type that needs to be constantly surrounded by people, I have discovered that there is a vast difference between choosing to spend time alone and being forced to do so. It is an entirely different scenario when one is thrust into a situation that resembles solitary confinement. Here I felt like a prisoner. Being in the body cast was like wearing shackles.

I wanted so badly to get up and walk, to be able

to do things for myself, to resume my life and get back to normal. But despite the fact that I believed that I would walk again, a little voice was telling me that my life would probably never be *normal* again. It was difficult to suppress those thoughts. I spent a lot of time reading and praying in an attempt to keep my mind occupied.

I can't speak for most people, but my brain doesn't process multiple things very well at the same time. So I figured that as long as I could keep positive thinking going on, then I could keep the negative from creeping in.

I spent many hours each day lifting weights and doing chin-ups on the trapeze bar on the hospital bed. I was going to need all of the upper-body strength I could get when I got to rehab. A few evenings a week, my brothers would put me through a rigorous workout. Pop had built a set of parallel bars so I could work on my standing endurance. My brothers would lift me up and stand me at the bars, and I would hold on for as long as I could so my body would start getting used to being vertical again.

As the days went by, I was beginning to move some muscles in my hips and legs that had been dormant, so I was becoming hopeful about walking. Unfortunately, I couldn't do a lot with many of the muscles while wearing that cast. So I would just push against the cast and do resistance exercises. (I'm sure trainers have a technical word for that.)

It was disappointing, however, that I still had no motor activity in my ankles or feet. I was going to need that in order to walk. Would those muscles come back? Why did I have to wait so long to get out of this darn cast? Would I really walk again? What would the rest of my life be like? Why had I been given this cross to bear?

I had more questions than I have space to write them. While I tried to remain focused and keep a positive attitude, the plain and simple truth is that I was angry. And I wasn't just a little angry. I didn't deserve this at all.

Looking back, I think I was being just a little selfish since, after all, who does deserve this? When I look around at all of the people I have known throughout my life, even those who have done me wrong, I can't think of one person about whom I would say, "They deserved this more than me." This was just the way the cards had been dealt at that point in my life. And I had a simple choice—either play the hand that I was dealt or fold, and I couldn't allow myself to fold.

I found peace and tranquility when I spent time outdoors. All I needed was to be lifted into the reclined wheelchair and rolled outside, and I was a happy camper. As it was middle to late autumn, the temperature was a little more bearable, and I could be comfortable. Early on, when it was warmer, I couldn't stay out too long in the sun, as I would begin to overheat in the cast and perspire and then start to itch. Anybody who has ever worn a cast knows what that is like.

I would close my eyes and let my mind wander.

Some of my most fond memories of growing up were of autumn. Autumn was harvest time, and the air smelled and felt different. As kids we would rake leaves into piles so big that we could get lost in them. It meant that winter was coming, and we would be able to ice skate when the pond would freeze. They were wonderful times.

As I lay there, I would breathe in the crisp autumn air, listen to the stream rolling by, and hear the deer running through the woods. In my mind, I was transported back to when I would revel in the activities of that very time of year. I found myself at peace.

After what seemed like an eternity, December 3, 1990, arrived. It was time to go back to the cast room at Jefferson Hospital and visit Tony, his sense of humor, and his cast saw. I was elated. I was going to be out of this cast forever! Well, Tony was cracking jokes the whole time and teasing me about when I first got the cast. (I had sort of whined a little at the time.) Tony is a black man, and when he got me up on the table, he plugged in his saw, turned it on, got it right up close to me, and said "All right, boy, now what about that contribution to the NAACP?"

I must have looked horrified as I stared at that buzzing saw while I weighed my options, because next thing I heard was Tony howling. I thought he was going to split his sides laughing. He was a great guy. Whether he was putting a cast on or removing it, he had a way of lightening up the moment. It only took a few minutes of cutting, and there I was, like a turtle out of its shell. I tipped the scales at a diminutive 115 pounds. Looking back, I think I actually needed help to tip the scale! I had lost forty pounds and looked like a refugee.

I was anxious to get down to business and start rehabilitation. I had managed to build some standing tolerance while in the body cast with people assisting me, but now that it was off, the sky was the limit. Before I was allowed to sit up, they put me in a brace that was basically a corset with steel ribs in it. My back wasn't stable enough yet for me to be moving around without support. So I accepted it semi-cheerfully (as if I had a choice!).

And so, I was off to my next stop on this journey, the rehabilitation hospital. The future held more character-building moments in store.

Off to Rehab

I rolled up into my sister Patricia's van in my rented wheelchair, only partially sitting up. After spending almost three months in the body cast, the muscles in my torso were so tight from inactivity that I couldn't bend far enough to sit up straight. Pop had built a ramp so the wheelchair could roll in and out of the van easily. Pop was an engineer's engineer. I mean, when he built something, you couldn't blow it up if you wanted to. We could have rolled a limousine up this ramp, so I felt quite safe at 115 pounds with my clunky wheelchair.

As we drove away, I watched Jefferson Hospital fade into the distance. I was closing one door and on my way to open another. I was beginning a new chapter. Less than a mile away was Magee Rehabilitation Hospital, my next stop on the tour.

I had visited Magee a month before while still in my cast so the staff there could do a physical evaluation. I had received a brief orientation but was still uncertain about what to expect. I was in new surroundings, with new people, and about to find out what I was made of. The fact is that we as human beings are not comfortable with change. And we all deal with it differently. Every day was an education. I was learning lessons about human nature, life, courage, faith, and patience.

My first surprise came when I signed all of the necessary paperwork for admission. One of the forms that I had to sign was an agreement that I would leave when I was discharged. I couldn't, for the life of me, imagine why this was necessary. Who would want to stay in a hospital? I had already had my fill, and I still was nowhere near the finish line.

I assured the nice lady in the admissions office that when they said, "Leave," the only parts of me they would see were going to be my backside and elbows as I went through the exit door. She said nothing and gave me a sour look that told me she was serious, so I politely smiled and signed the form. Welcome to Magee Rehab. I was making new friends already!

I was taken to this rather large room and was immediately impressed. It had a king-size bed as well as a large color television. I had stayed in hotels that weren't this nice. Oh baby, I had finally hit pay dirt. *All that time with four patients in a room, and now I'm at this resort,* I thought to myself.

We've all heard the saying that if it sounds too good to be true, it probably is. You've heard that, right? Well, it's a fact. This was what was known as the family room. It was available for family members to use if they needed to stay over and was only going to be mine for a night or so. Once a regular bed became available, I would be put in with the general population. Oh well, I lived in luxury for a few days.

I still was hoping that this was all just a bad dream. I couldn't walk, I couldn't sit up straight, and I couldn't even tie my own shoes. I was running out of patience. I figured that I must have really ticked God off.

My first night one of the doctors came in to see me. If my life depended on it, I couldn't remember her name; however, she left an indelible mark that I've never forgotten. I talked about my goals and informed her that I intended to be walking by the time I was discharged. Her response was, "Well, I wouldn't hold my breath if I were you." A punch in the face would have been easier to accept.

But she actually did me a favor since, as I mentioned once, I'm just a little hardheaded. I'm not rebellious by nature (I'm working on it though!), but being told that I can't do something doesn't sit very well. I made it my mission to prove her wrong.

What I really wanted right at that moment though was a shower. I had been in that body cast for months and wasn't feeling my best. One of the nurses put me on a shower trolley so I could remain flat, as I was not allowed to sit up without my corset on. The feel of the hot water and soap was fabulous. I had forgotten what it was like. We take so many simple things for granted, like long hot showers. I soon felt like a brand-new man.

In the next day or so, I met the members of my treatment team. The team consisted of my doctors, a physical therapist, an occupational therapist, a social worker, and a psychologist. I was not shy about stating my position of what I thought I could accomplish. I really didn't want any part of the psychology bit; however, it was part of the program. So I figured that I may as well play nicely for the time being. I was given my schedule, and it was to consist of two sessions of physical therapy and two sessions of occupational therapy each day, as well as a weekly visit to the psychologist.

In addition, there would be a group psychology session on Thursday afternoons in place of one of my physical therapy sessions. My first thought was *group psychology?*

Uh oh, we need to talk. I wasn't really keen on the idea of sitting in a room full of strangers and introducing myself. "Hi, I'm Bob, and I'm—blah, blah, blah."

And they wanted me to give up a physical therapy session to do it? It made for some interesting discussions. I went to "group" sometimes but was much happier in the gym working on getting stronger. My goal was to walk again, and I wanted to devote all my time to that, not to listening to the problems of strangers.

In retrospect, I regret that decision in some ways. I was hardheaded enough to simply plow ahead and do what I needed to do, not taking the time to realize that maybe some people needed guidance and support. It's possible that I may have been able to make a difference to some of those people but chose not to. For that I am sorry.

There was quite a diverse mix of people that made up the patient population. I met people from all walks of life and all age groups, and each had their own unique situation that had brought them there. Some I recognized from being at Jefferson, while others were new to me. I caught up with Keith, who had been transferred there before I was. He had been working hard to become independent of the ventilator, and while he was making progress, the outlook wasn't promising. He was on my mind a lot, as he was such a nice man.

The more I met and talked with other patients, I was beginning to understand quickly why they had psychologists on the staff. None of us was there by choice, but it saddened me to see some that were as bitter and angry as they were. I think in some cases it stifled their ability to fight for recovery.

I knew how important it was going to be that I continue to stay positive. I was beginning to get more of an education than I ever thought possible, not just about other people, but also myself. Despite my determination and progress, I still had the little voice of uncertainty talking to me from time to time. But I knew I could beat it.

Christmas arrived, and I was able to get a day pass so I could spend Christmas with my family. I went to my parents' house for the day, as it has always been and still is the general gathering place on holidays. I was happy to be out in the real world, if for just a day. I was not able to walk yet, so everything required a wheelchair. But it was nice to be around all of my family at one time and eat some real everyday food.

I convinced my father to take me to a nearby industrial park so I could try driving. To say that it was a strange experience would be an understatement. I had a minimal amount of movement in my hips and knees, but I couldn't feel or move my feet or even bend my ankles at all—they just kind of flopped around, making it difficult to gauge how hard I was pushing on the pedals. There wasn't anything smooth about my driving that day, but I viewed the mission as successful since I hadn't hit anything.

Unfortunately, the day was too brief, and shortly after dinner I had to return to the hospital. I had only been there for three weeks so far and was looking forward to being discharged. I just had to learn how to walk first.

My physical therapist, Margie Roos, continued to push me to my limits. She knew how determined I was to walk again and was behind me all the way. Amazingly, not everyone was as supportive, including a few staff members. Too often in life, we hear people say things such as "It's not good to get your hopes up," or "We don't want to see you get disappointed," or the one that I heard the most, "The sooner you accept your situation, the better off you'll be." Yes, in the eyes of many, I was in denial of my condition.

While I understand that they had seen many patients with spinal-cord injuries come through the system, they didn't know *me*. I didn't believe for a minute that my goals were unrealistic or not possible. Remember, I'm hardheaded. It didn't take long before I dreaded the psychology sessions, especially the one-on-one meetings. At least at group, I could blend in and just be a spectator. When I met with the psychologist alone, she sort of expected me to participate in the conversation. I had never been one to bare my soul to a total stranger and wasn't really in the mood to start at that point. But I quickly realized two things. First, the more that I didn't want to talk, the more she thought there was something really wrong. That, of course, made her ask more questions like, "Well, just how does this make you feel?" or "Why can't you accept your situation?" There really wasn't any big crisis; I just didn't want to talk. I was tired of explaining to people that I wasn't in denial. I was simply determined to walk. The second thing I realized was that I wasn't going to get out of going to these meetings. They took a dim view of those who didn't go "by the book"; they labeled those patients as uncooperative. So, I just had to decide to make it fun.

While there were several psychologists on staff, Keith and I had been assigned to the same one. It turned out he felt the same way I did and that we also had similar views on many things in life. It also turned out that Dr. Smith had radically different views and made the mistake of letting it be known. I assure you that at election time she did not pull the same lever on voting machines as Keith and me. We had found her Achilles' heel!

So Keith and I devised a plan. Every week we would decide ahead of time what we would talk about in our therapy sessions. Miraculously, we ended up with the shortest sessions of anybody there. All we had to do was turn to any political topic, and the meeting was over!

Now understand that Keith, as a quadriplegic, had little movement in his hands. One day at one of his sessions, he told Dr. Smith that my brother brought him one of my guns so he could practice pulling the trigger to strengthen his fingers. She shrieked and immediately ended his session.

Now there are two things that I need to be clear about. First of all, no gun was ever given to Keith. I would never be a party to such a thing. Secondly, I had no knowledge ahead of time that he was going to pull that one. But I sure caught some flak over it though!

The funniest part of the whole thing was watching him trying to tell me the story. He was so proud of himself for pulling a fast one on the doctor, and he was laughing so hard and couldn't catch his breath very well, as he still had the tracheotomy. On a good day, it was hard to understand Keith when he tried to speak, and now he was hysterical. It was hard to tell if he was laughing or gasping for breath. The truth is we really weren't trying to be mean. Honest. We simply were growing bored and tired of the daily monotonous routine of hospital life, and we figured that if we didn't liven things up some, we might crack up and need to see a psychologist, which, by the way, we were obviously trying to avoid doing in the first place! Eventually Dr. Smith finally realized we were simply razzing her a little, and we got along just fine. Sort of.

As my legs got stronger, Margie decided it was time for me to try taking some steps. I started out in the parallel bars, with Margie behind me and a big strap around my waist in case I fell. I made it through the bars but was exhausted and had to sit down. I was very unstable, as many of the muscles in my hips and legs were still not functioning. As a result, I was relying on just a few muscles to do all of the work. I still had no motor activity in the lower parts of my legs, in my ankles, and in my feet. It weighed heavily on me, as I would not be able to walk effectively or safely in that condition.

But I continued to work with what I had and do the exercises Margie gave me with only one exception. If she told me to do an exercise twenty times, I did it forty times. I wanted this program to be on the fast track. I had prayed for strength and help, but as the saying goes, God helps those who help themselves.

I was starting to see the results of my work, and those results were enabling me to have greater faith and belief. It was happening—I was getting up out of the wheelchair! True, sometimes I would lose my balance and fall, but I kept getting back up. I had a deadline to meet. I needed to walk out of the hospital and had committed myself since I told everybody I was going to. There was no turning back. I was taking steps, and my dream was becoming reality!

Unfortunately, this led to a hard lesson, which is that the world has a lot of people who just can't wait to rain on your parade. A number of the other patients began making a lot of unpleasant comments, subtle things, like, "Who does he think he is?" or "What are you trying to prove?" A few even laughed when I would fall.

It reminds me of the story of Joseph in the Bible. The book of Genesis tells us of Joseph having a dream of greatness: that he would be a leader. His older brothers hated him since he was the favorite son and were angered even more at the thought of being led by him. They said, "Look, the dreamer is coming. Come therefore, let us now kill him" (Genesis 37:19–20). They stripped him of his tunic of many colors, cast him into a well, and ultimately sold him into slavery. Looking back, I would say that I got off relatively easy. I was only being ridiculed.

But I had my own tunic of many colors that I wore, so to speak, and that was my pride and determination. And I was not going to let anybody strip me of it. I did feel fairly confident that there wasn't much chance I would be thrown into a well, as many of the patients were in worse shape than I was. But I could have done without the comments.

I have found that there are many reasons that people may try to dissuade another from reaching their goal. Oftentimes it is out of jealousy or laziness. They are not willing to do what you are attempting to do, so therefore, they don't want you to be successful. You will make them look bad. They are comfortable where they are, as long as they are surrounded with similar-thinking people.

I've often referred to this scenario as the "crab theory." If you ever watch a basket of live crabs, every time one tries to climb out, one of the other crabs pulls it back down. It's almost as if the one crab is saying, "You're going down like the rest of us, my friend!" One of the patients actually said to me, "So you really think you're going to walk? Face it; you're crippled like the rest of us." I felt sorry for him; I truly did. I believe he would have had the possibility to progress from where he was, but he allowed his anger and bitterness over his injury to consume him.

Sometimes, the people who try to hold us back are those that are close to us. They care about us and don't want to see us get hurt. This is often difficult to deal with because we know that they love us and care about us. But we cannot allow them to derail us. The bottom line is that if you have a dream or goal, stick to it and fight for it. Don't quit!

Fortunately, a few patients saw my progress as inspiration. Keith was one of my biggest fans, and we would feed off of one another's positive energy. What impressed me the most about him was the fact that his case was so severe, and he kept his spirits up better than many. He was a true champion.

I had transitioned to using a walker, but I had reached a plateau. Many of the muscles in my legs still weren't responding because of the nerve damage in my spinal cord, and I was very unstable when standing. My legs and hips would wobble all over the place when I tried to stand or walk. It was so bad that one day Margie asked me if I wanted some fries with my "shake." Did I mention the importance of having a sense of humor?

I just had to be patient as I waited for things to heal. Nerves do regenerate, but it is a slow process, and I'm not very good at waiting for things. That's probably why I was never much of a hunter. It involves the three things that I dislike the most: getting up early, sitting in the cold, and *waiting!* Margie and I discussed my options and concluded that braces on my legs would help. This had definitely not been in my plans, but it would get the job done. Molds were taken of my legs, since the braces must be custom made to fit each patient. So in the meantime, I continued to work hard to build my strength and endurance while I waited for my braces to be made.

I found it more and more difficult to be patient the closer I got to my goal. I think most of the people handling my case had figured out that I meant business and that I was not going to just sit by and accept what came my way. I began to see a positive change in some who had viewed my goals as unrealistic.

One of the doctors involved in my case happened to be in a wheelchair herself. She was a great lady, and we were of similar personalities. She always kept me on my toes. One day she told me that they were going to be changing one of my bladder medications.

Being the ever inquisitive one and always full of questions, I naturally asked why. She looked me straight in the eye and said, "The medication you are currently taking has been found to cause cancer in laboratory rats, and being the rat that you are, we felt you might be at high risk." Ouch!

Try as she could, it was no longer possible for her to keep a straight face. Of course, I knew she was kidding. I always welcomed her unique sense of humor, as I often felt that I had met my match whenever we would exchange wits. I respected her positions and opinions on many issues, as I felt that she knew firsthand many of the issues that patients faced, and I could easily talk to this doctor about pretty much anything, medical or otherwise. I figured that anybody who could trade barbs like she could had to be okay.

I continued to struggle with many obstacles. Despite the fact that I was beginning to take steps, I was still dependent on the wheelchair. Despite my best efforts to be careful, I still had some skin and infection issues. And try as I might, sometimes I had difficulty keeping my head in the game. The mind is an amazing thing, but it is a constant battle to keep it on track when dealing with so many unfamiliar things. I was not accustomed to spending large periods of time idle. And in this environment, I almost felt trapped. I couldn't go anywhere, so I had to rely on family or friends to bring me anything I needed. Sometimes, I almost took it personally if they had not had the time or had simply forgotten to pick up an item I had requested.

I would build model airplanes to help pass the time and had asked Jack to pick up some more paint for me. He showed up the next evening without the paint, as his schedule had not permitted him to get to the hobby store to buy it. I was crushed! How could my own brother let me down? I did my best to not let my emotions show, and looking back I realize how foolish I was being.

I was often amazed and even embarrassed that small things could get to me the way they did. I have never understood how people get released from prison and do something to get sent back. Just two months of being trapped inside those four walls were enough for me, and there wasn't even a barbed-wire fence. I was starting to go a little buggy, and it bothered me. I couldn't wait to get out of there. Of course, I can say all of this now. If I had admitted it back then, they would have made me see the psychologist, and then Keith and I would have gotten in more trouble.

But at that point, my world consisted of several therapy sessions each day, mealtime, and any way I chose to fill the remainder of the day. I was never much of a television watcher, so I built my models and read books. There was a large room with a wide-screen television and VCR so we could watch movies. One night everybody decided we should watch the movie *Airplane,* in honor of me wrecking one. Everybody was a comedian. Fortunately, growing up in a large family, I'm not thin-skinned.

When we reached the absolute pinnacle of boredom, we would line up and flip our wheelchairs back on to two wheels so we were reclined against the wall and sit there and shoot the breeze about absolutely nothing. We looked like a bunch of old men sitting out in front of the hardware store, except that quite often the girls joined us too. They were just as bored as we were.

They didn't do wheelies though; I guess it's pretty much a guy thing. I had just gotten my new wheelchair and really thought that I was the bomb. It was red, low-slung, sleek-looking, and lightweight. It had ball-bearing hubs and was fast. Look out, world—I was ready for Talladega! Only "newbies" cruise around in those ugly chrome, heavy, rental wheelchairs. I was somebody now, or so I thought. One night I was being cool (once again, so I thought), was popping wheelies, and went right over backwards, whacking my head on a railing. All I could think was, *Well, that didn't turn out too good. Anybody got a bandage?* I received a stern butt-chewing from one of the nurses, and I vowed not to do wheelies anymore. Yeah, sure I wouldn't.

I was so bored at one point that I even read the Warren Report. Now that was some dry reading! To this day, I'm still not sure who assassinated President Kennedy, but I think it was Mrs. Peacock, in the conservatory, with the revolver. But I could be wrong. Next time I feel like boring myself to tears, I'll reread it and check my facts. But it passed the time.

Fortunately, there would occasionally be some random incident that put us into stitches laughing. One night, this one particular patient had called for the nurse to help him. Bill was a quadriplegic and, as such, was unable to get himself out of his wheelchair and into bed, so the nurse went to lift him and make the transfer. Now it is important to understand that this nurse was extremely buxom. I mean, *a lot* buxom.

Well, long story short, it was as hot as the Sahara that night in the hospital, and before lifting Bill into the bed, the nurse decided to take off her sweater. Did I mention that it was a pullover? Yeah, you already guessed it, didn't you? She went to whip the sweater off and unknowingly took her blouse with it. She threw the garments on the table, leaned over, cradled Bill right up tight against her, picked him up, put him in his bed, and *then* realized that she had no blouse on. That poor boy got an eyeful and a face full; he was never the same. For the rest of his hospital stay, he kind of had this permanent goofy look on his face.

And then to add insult to injury, we got him again a few nights later. Jack showed up for a visit with one of his harem. He couldn't hang this one on me, since he actually showed up with her. I think her name was Babette or Cupcake, or maybe Twinkie. Yeah, Twinkie, that was it. Well anyway, they were on their way to some place fancy, so she was dressed in some little, short, sparkling party dress. And unfortunately for Bill, he chose this precise time to ring for the nurse to help him into his bed. Yes, once again, timing was everything.

Well, Nurse Buxom happened to be in my room at the time (with her blouse on), and we all said, "Let's send Twinkie instead." So we all scrambled down the hall in our wheelchairs to see the show as she pranced into Bill's room and exclaimed, "Hi, I'm Twinkie, and I'm here to put you to bed!" His eyes dang near popped right out of his head. All he could say was, "Who—who—who—?" I guess he was trying to say, "Who are you?" I suppose we'll never know. By the time he was discharged, he had a permanent goofy look *and* a stuttering problem.

But then the funny antics would end, and we would all go back to reality and listen to one another talk about nothing much. Everybody had a story about how they came to be there, and it was always someone else's fault. Each of them was going to be a millionaire when their lawyer filed and settled their case. I knew better. But I let them tell their stories anyway. Sometimes listening to all of the heartaches made it tough to stay on track mentally, and I would just find a place to be alone for a while.

There was a particularly rough and colorful group whom we referred to as the "gunshot gang." This was a group of inner-city fellows that were paralyzed as a result of gunshot wounds. They all claimed to be innocent, and they all claimed that they didn't know who had shot them. But all of them were very adamant that when they got out of the hospital they were going to get the son-of-a-you-know-what who had shot them. We read about these things in the newspaper and see them on the news every day, but it was sad to see it firsthand. There was a fair amount of bitterness that surrounded this group, and despite efforts to tune it out, it sometimes ended up being a distraction. It was just one more part of the big picture.

Financial issues weighed heavily on my mind. I was getting phone calls in my hospital room from one of the previous hospitals that had treated me. They wanted to discuss payment of my bills for portions that had not been covered by the insurance company. Were they kidding? I was still in the hospital! I couldn't allow these issues to derail me at that point, so I put an answering machine in my hospital room. It was my full intention to address those matters, but I had to deal with the most important issue, which was to get better, walk out of the hospital, and not leave in a wheelchair.

I did receive a phone call from the service manager at the dealership. Joe asked if I could get a set of my keys to him so he could move my tools to a storage area until I was ready to come back. Things were looking better already. I believed that I was going to get better, and obviously some other people did too.

Jack took care of dropping my keys off to the dealership. My tools would be safe, and I was feeling some security knowing that I would be able to return to work when I was ready. After all, these people were my friends, right? Many had been to visit me, and I knew that they cared. At least finances would not be a grave concern, so I could concentrate on my recovery.

Unfortunately, I received some paperwork a week or so later indicating that the workman compensation claim had been denied and that I had been *terminated*. That word has such a negative ring to it. In fact, the date of termination listed on the paperwork predated Joe's phone call about getting the keys for my tools. Whether or not he was aware of the termination, I will never know, but I wouldn't doubt it. I was in shock. All of my so-called friends had developed a serious case of amnesia about the fact that the event had been company sponsored. They had all been present at the monthly meeting when the owner of the dealership and his son made the announcement. I had trusted these people. And now they had keys to my toolboxes. This was not good.

I had to lean on Jack again. I asked him to take his truck, pick up all of my tools, and put them in the garage at my apartment. It wasn't until I got home and went through them that I realized my tools had really been picked over. It was obvious that Joe had not kept my keys in a secure place, and others had helped themselves to whatever they wanted in my toolboxes. I had just learned another of life's valuable lessons: keep your friends close and your enemies closer! But I had to keep moving on toward the goal at hand.

In the meantime, my leg braces arrived, and I was eager to put them on and try to walk. They took getting used to, as they basically held my ankle and foot in a fixed position. Now I was going to be going places! Actually, I was going places as long as those places were close by. My endurance level was still insufficient to cover a lot of ground, and my balance, while better with the braces, was still lacking. So I continued to trip and fall from time to time. But the important thing was that I continued to get up each time I fell, and I would practice walking every chance I had. Margie only had one rule, and it was that I was not allowed to attempt walking without supervision. Two nursing supervisors would take some time in the evenings and on weekends to walk with me up and down the hallway.

One of the supervisors, Sherry, was planning to walk with me one day, and I tried to stand up before she was next to me. And wouldn't you know it; I fell flat on my face. It wasn't her fault, as I should have waited for her, but she felt just awful. The next day, there were four boxes of Girl Scout cookies on my bed along with a note from her. I volunteered to throw myself on the floor daily if it would get me a constant supply Samoas and Thin Mints, my two favorite varieties. She was a great lady and really made my time there bearable. She was active in the Air Force Reserves and used to regale me with stories of her times airborne in C-141 transport aircraft. Being a pilot, I would listen to anything having to do with airplanes. I was truly blessed to have crossed paths with her on my journey.

The other supervisor happened to be nine-months pregnant at the time. She used to lean me up against her belly, say, "Let's go," and walk me until I couldn't go any farther. I would go thirty or forty feet, stop to sit down and rest, and then go some more.

I prayed that she didn't go into labor while walking with me! I enjoyed the time I spent with those two sweet ladies. They believed in me, and their encouragement went a long way in helping me strive for my goals. The end was in sight and I was excited.

It wasn't too much longer until Margie told me that the "team" had met and scheduled my discharge date as February 19, 1991. I was not aware that it showed, but a change came over me. Margie tells me that it was obvious.

Someone once described the term *mixed emotions* to me as watching your mother-in-law drive off a cliff—in *your* new car! Well, I don't know that my feelings were that extreme, but I was discovering mixed emotions of my own. While I couldn't wait to leave, I had discovered that the hospital environment that I had known for many months, while monotonous, tedious, and sometimes downright irritating, was a very secure environment.

My mind flashed back to the day that I signed in and that form I had signed agreeing to leave when discharged. Believe me when I tell you that a team of Clydesdales could not have dragged me back into this environment. I was leaving. But I now understood why they made people sign that form. I had heard stories of patients who just wouldn't leave, as they had no place to go or were simply afraid of what lay ahead of them. Ahead of me was the daunting task of doing everything on my own and trying to fit into society, into the "real world."

You see, I would now have to do everything for myself. I had just moved into a new apartment when I had my accident. Getting to the apartment required two flights of stairs. Everything I owned was still in boxes. I was going to have to shop for myself, cook my own meals, and figure out how I was going to pay for it all. I was now unemployed, as my so-called friends had terminated me before they even knew what my condition would ultimately be. I kind of saw it coming, as they had all stopped calling and visiting.

I had successfully driven a car, but I was going to have to retest to keep my license. I would have to face people and wonder if they would accept me in my current condition. In the hospital everyone was either handicapped or an employee that worked with the handicapped. It was a very non-threatening existence from a psychological standpoint. It was becoming apparent that I was not destined to make a full recovery, with some of the residual issues being of a more personal nature. How would I ever fit into society? Would people understand? Trepidation had set in.

One of the final steps in the process before discharge is a home visit. Basically, select members of the team go out with the patient to their home to make sure

that all accommodations in the residence are acces-
sible and that the patient can get around safely when
home. This was probably one of their more unique
visits, as I wasn't even unpacked from moving. Not
all of the utilities were in operation yet, and they
couldn't believe that I was planning to go home and
live alone in a second-floor apartment.

Added to the mix was that I wasn't exactly real
steady on my feet yet. They were convinced that I
was crazy. But that was all right, because one thing
that I have learned is that if you don't have someone
telling you that you are crazy, then your goal isn't
big enough. If someone doesn't doubt your ability,
it means that you are fitting into their world and
probably downsizing your goal. And the only world
I cared about fitting into at that point was mine. My
goals, my dreams—that's it.

I really wasn't excited about doing this home-
visit thing, but I figured that, once again, I might as
well play nicely with the other kids, the kids in this
case being hospital staff. I am certain that I made
them all quite nervous trying to negotiate two flights
of stairs, one of which had no railing. Once in the
apartment, they basically just wanted to see that I
could get around, reach everything, and get into the
shower safely without breaking my back (again),
basically seeing if I could do all of my "ADLs". The
day wasn't too painful, and I somehow convinced the
"team" that I would be fine on my own in the apartment. Of course, it's not as if they were going to keep
me; I was getting discharged and going home—win,
lose, or draw!

February 19 arrived quicker than I could have imagined. I still recall the event like it was yesterday. Probably the most accurate comparison I can make would be likening it to graduation day. I had worked hard and paid my dues, and it was time to say good-bye to "staff and underclassmen and other gradu-ates." Several other patients I had come to know also had discharge dates close to mine. And like gradua-tion, or even a class reunion, we swore that we would keep in touch. And of course we know what really happens there. But there were some people that I would miss, and there were some that I *had* to leave behind. I packed most of my belongings the night before, and believe me, I had accumulated quite a bit in the lengthy time that I had been there. Some of my airplane models had taken a turn for the worst. I had them hanging from the ceiling in my room on display, and at one point a nurse had come in during the night and demolished some of them. It was dark, and she saw things in the air with wings and thought that they were bats!

She screamed, took a swing, and wiped a few of them out. Oh well, a few less things to worry about packing. I didn't bother to ask her how she ever thought that bats would have gotten into my hospi-tal room or how they would be hovering motionless. Some things are just better left alone.

I didn't sleep a lot that night, but it wasn't a bad or restless lack of sleep. I just had many things on my mind and actually felt a certain kind of peace over me. I had gone the distance, so to speak, and now it was time to move on. And while there was some trepidation about the immediate future, I was okay.

Granted, I still had a long way to go. In addition to wearing the leg braces, I used forearm crutches to hold myself up. Really, the only way to describe my gait was that I didn't have one. My walking consisted more of putting my weight on the forearm crutches and swinging my legs forward one at a time. I was not graceful, and I was still skinny as a rail—it's difficult to pack on the pounds with hospital food. I was quite a sight! But I felt pretty good about everything.

God had been watching over me up until this point, and I knew that I would continue to be safe in His hands. I had set a goal; I had faced the challenge head-on and was going to accomplish that goal. In just a few hours, I would walk out of the hospital, walking badly, but I would be walking out.

When morning arrived, I was a little weary but felt like a little kid on Christmas morning. My big day was here. After breakfast I made one last trip through the hospital to say good-bye. While I was scheduled to come back for outpatient physical therapy, there were a few people I wouldn't see again.

My last stop was to see the doctor that I had met on my first night there. She was the one who told me not to hold my breath when it came to walking again. While I had used my wheelchair to make my rounds through the rest of the hospital, I made certain that I was up on my feet when I saw her. I couldn't go very far and was using leg braces and crutches, but I was walking.

The purpose of my visit was to thank her. I told her that I couldn't imagine why she would have said such a thing, but her words only served as further incentive to accomplish my goal. If nothing else, I had to prove her wrong. Perhaps that was her intention. Either way, I was grateful.

My New Life

I had spent the last five months basically rebuilding my body and now had to begin the task of rebuilding my life. I was in a new second-floor apartment, still had most of my belongings in boxes, had no furniture, and had been terminated from my job. And given my physical condition, I was not exactly a real desirable commodity. I did not have good balance; couldn't stand for long periods of time; was still wearing the corset to support my back, which prevented me from bending; and couldn't lift anything of any substance. Being a mechanic requires all of these things.

It had been a goal of mine to open my own shop, but it was quite evident that my days as an auto mechanic were over. That is not meant to sound pessimistic, but the reality was that I could have risked further injury by pushing my body beyond the limitations that I now faced. I just had to be practical about all of this. When I thought about all that I was facing, it seemed a bit overwhelming. But, as the old saying goes about how to eat an elephant, you do it one bite at a time. Besides, God hadn't let me down yet, and I knew He would stand by me. So I started with one task at a time in order of priority. I began to get the apartment into shape a little at a time, as everything took me longer to do than before. Speed and stamina were not my strong points, but fortunately I wasn't in a hurry. Pop has always reminded me to recognize the difference between the things that we can or cannot control.

I continued to do physical therapy on an outpatient basis. And while I was making gains, they were happening in small increments. Someone had told me that it would probably be a year before I would feel like a human being again. I was beginning to believe it. I was going to have to wear the corset for at least two more months to be sure that my spine was completely healed and stable. A lot of muscles were still stiff, and many of the muscles in my legs that no longer worked anymore had been affected by atrophy. This of course meant that my leg braces didn't fit properly anymore, so I had to have new ones made.

Fortunately, I was able to drive, even though I still needed to retest. Whenever a person suffers any neurological disorder, the hospital sends a letter to the motor vehicle department stating the person's condition and that it "*may* affect their ability to safely operate a vehicle." The state didn't take away my license but simply put it under what is termed "non-renewable status." When it came time to renew my license, I couldn't simply send in the form and payment as before. I needed to go to the driver testing center and go through the whole test again to make sure I could safely operate the vehicle.

This was rather interesting, as I was not able and cannot to this day move at all or feel much of anything in my feet and lower parts of my legs. Suffice to say that there was no way I wanted to be putting hand controls in my car. So I had to use a little "smoke and mirrors" to get through the test, but I made it, and my paperwork was forwarded to the DMV in Harrisburg. Of course, having the luck of the Irish, my paperwork was lost, and it took several months to resolve it, leaving me without a valid license. It was just another one of those little curve balls being pitched at me.

I finally did receive my new license, and interestingly enough, the state had taken away the endorsement to drive trucks since I had only retested in a car but left the motorcycle endorsement in place. Who knows what they were thinking? Not that it really mattered anyway. After all, would a gimpy guy be crazy enough to try riding a motorcycle or try driving a tractor trailer? But I suppose that I better not talk about that on the grounds that it might incriminate me!

In between my physical therapy sessions, I was working a few hours a week for a friend I had known for many years. Dean Keyes owned a local towing and auto-repair shop and needed someone to help out in the office. Looking back, I'm not sure whether or not he simply created the position. He had been like a brother over the years and had always cared about me and knew that I needed to get back out into the world. It had really been weighing heavily on my mind as to how people would accept me in mainstream society. After all, I was *different* now and had been keeping to myself. It didn't require a second thought, and I quickly welcomed Dean's invitation. While I was not accustomed to office work, I had to accept the fact that I now had some limitations. I had worked for Dean back in the eighties, and while I knew the business inside and out, working on large trucks and driving car carriers cross-country just wasn't in the cards anymore. So I resorted to exciting things, like billing and scheduling vehicle transports—things that would keep me from hurting myself.

Although I was able to get up on my feet and walk short distances, I still had to wear the braces and use the crutches, and I had an absolutely awful and unstable gait and was extremely self-conscious. The truth is that I was being my own biggest obstacle. But at the time, I didn't know what to expect from people, so I expected the worst. However, most people just treated me like anyone else.

As time went on, I worked on adjusting to my situation and met many new people. I had broken ties with a lot of people that I had known prior to my accident, not necessarily by choice. In many cases, they did it for me. I had learned a hard lesson about the difference between friends and acquaintances. Many people are your so-called friend when times are good and you're buying a round at happy hour. But when the stuffing hits the fan, people begin to show what they are made of. Unfortunately, as a result of this, I had become a little more cautious when it came to allowing people to get too close to me too soon. In the many years since, I've worked hard at getting through that, as I realize that most people we encounter day to day are truly good people. I had simply been let down by some people that I thought were friends and allowed that to cloud my judgment when it came to others. I had forgotten about all of those who had stepped up to the plate and were wonderful to me. I found myself to be looking at the glass as half empty instead of half full. I needed to change that, as I was focusing on myself. I discovered that it was better to focus on the people I met and simply smile and be myself.

I realized that I needed to continue with the attitude that I had maintained throughout my time in the hospital. I could not allow any negativity to creep in and affect my progress. I needed to set new goals and then strive to reach them. Granted, there were many things that I couldn't do anymore, and it was frustrating to have to rely on others to help me. But I had to keep trying. It has often been said that whether you think you can or whether you think you can't, you're right. I know that this is true no matter what we face in life. Every problem contains its own solution; we just need to look for it.

I needed more confidence, and the only way I saw to acquire it was to achieve greater results. I had gotten to the point where I didn't use the crutches anymore and was using canes. I still would occasionally use my wheelchair if I had to cover any distance, but those were isolated instances.

I was getting more comfortable with life in general and spent some time at the beach with Jack. He was more than happy to turn over the driving duties on the boat to me, thereby giving me the nickname Captain Bob. I have some very funny memories of the summers at the beach in Stone Harbor, New Jersey. There's probably enough material there alone for a book, truly a unique atmosphere. I had begun playing the guitar, which was something I had always wanted to do since I was young. I was learning to stop putting things off, as life is too short.

———

By the spring of 1993, I was feeling the urge to get back into an airplane. Mostly, I think that I just wanted to see if I could do it, if I could get back on the horse that had thrown me, so to speak. Of course, I was going to pick an airplane that was a little more substantial with better handling characteristics. You don't have to hit me in the head twice for me to learn something!

I came across a fellow that I hadn't seen since my days in Boy Scouts decades ago, who was now a flight instructor. I told Dan my story and said that basically I wanted to go up for a ride and see how it felt. Either he wasn't listening or perhaps knew what I really needed, because he gave me the pilot's seat and handed me the keys and the checklists. I was approaching all of this with an open mind, as I was fully aware that I might not have the same enthusiasm for flying as I once did.

It turned out to be one of the most exhilarating times I'd had in several years. It had been almost three years since I had flown (and crashed), but it felt almost as if I had flown the week before. My motions and procedures were fluid. Everything came back to me instantly, and I had a hard time believing that it had been so long since I had been at the controls of an airplane. I had a great time that day.

I flew with Dan two more times; however, I was not in a position to pursue more flying at that point. My condition would not permit me to pass the required physical, and the FAA had suspended my license after my accident. They get really cranky when you bend up an airplane, as they should. There is a little bit of pilot humor that states that any landing you can walk away from is a good one, and if the plane is still useable, the landing was a great one. Well, folks, I hadn't accomplished either one of those tasks, so the FAA decided that if I ever wanted to fly again, I would have to retest. That was going to have to wait, but I had proven to myself that I could still fly an airplane! There are few things that compare to the experience of flying an airplane and seeing the earth from up high as God sees it. It is truly breathtaking.

The year 1993 continued to be a turning point in my life as that is when I met Sharon.

I love telling this story to people, and I swear that *most* of it is true. There is a small town called Wawa, Pennsylvania, which has a dairy. The company, named for the town, also has a rather large chain of convenience stores covering several states. There happens to be one of these stores in downtown Media, near the towing company. Also in Media is a day care and child-development center with a beautiful lady as the director. As fate would have it, I often went into this store and so did Sharon. For several months I noticed her and would say hello, make small talk, and go on my way. She was such a sweet lady, with great legs too! I was smitten.

One thing that I did not know at the time is that the word *wawa* is the Lenape Indian word for goose. The next part is where our stories differ. I seem to recall learning this because Sharon explained it to me after she goosed (grabbed) me one day in the store and said she had to do so because we were in the *Wawa* store. She, of course, denies this completely. I'm simply pleading the fifth.

I finally decided that I better catch this girl before someone else did. But, naturally, I wondered if my physical condition would put her off. I was still walking with two canes and not doing a great job of it. It turned out to not be a big deal at all, as when she was describing me to her coworkers, Sharon said that she *thought* I might have had a cane but wasn't sure. To this day, I still admire her powers of observation!

Sharon and I met for dinner, and the more time I spent with her, the more I realized that we belonged together. I had never met anyone like her before and was not about to let her get away. We had some rather ironic similarities, such as Sharon losing her mother to cancer on September 9, the same date as my accident. It also turned out that my mother had known Sharon's father from high school. It sure is a small world! Sharon and I continued to spend much of our time together and build the foundation for what I knew was to become a lifelong relationship. It didn't take long before we were inseparable.

By spring of 1994, I was getting the itch to fly again. But truthfully, it was only something that I would pursue if Sharon had any interest. I had made the decision that she was going to be the top priority in my life. Over Memorial Day weekend, we stopped by the Chester County Airport while we were out running a few errands, and Sharon was genuinely interested in all of the various airplanes.

But what really caught her attention was the airplane that flew overhead and landed. It was a 1940ish Spartan Executive, and the sound was incredible. Any pilot, or for that matter, anyone with even a slight pulse, can appreciate the sound of a radial engine, and that's putting it mildly. (For any non-pilots, a radial is one of those "round" engines with the cylinders all in a circle.) In comparison, a Harley sounds like a windup toy. There's something about the sound of a radial engine that makes you grin from ear to ear.

We chatted only briefly with the pilot and his wife, as they were headed back out for more flying, but he told us to go ahead into his hangar and make ourselves at home. We waited until they took off again, as I didn't want Sharon to miss the sound of that airplane at full throttle on takeoff. We visited briefly with the man's son in the hangar and looked at the three other WWII vintage airplanes that he owned, a T-6, a P51D Mustang, and a Corsair, all of which were in pristine show condition.

We enjoyed our short visit, and the young boy gave us a photo of the Mustang, named *Big Beautiful Doll*, which was taken airborne while his father was flying it. Sharon just thought that all of this was the cat's pajamas. I figured that Sharon must have had flying in her blood since it took several hours to get the smile off of her face. She was hooked.

Shortly thereafter, she took a flight in a small plane and had the opportunity to take the controls. Sharon needed no persuasion and on August 7, 1994, took her first flight lesson at Brandywine Airport in West Chester. I was so proud of Sharon as she worked hard to study and practice. Learning to fly is not difficult, but there is a lot of material to learn and at times can appear to be a daunting task if one looks too far ahead in the training syllabus.

I assured Sharon that all she needed to do was start with the basics and then use each new skill as a building block. And then, when the more challenging tasks came along, they would be easier to master. It would turn out to be one of the most important concepts that Sharon had learned, as she would come to rely on it years later when fighting for her life.

Sharon really had a great time learning to fly in "four-triple-niner." It was a little red and white Cessna 152 that she really liked. Her instructor, Jimmy, was top notch. Not only did he have years of experience in both prop and jet aircraft, he was a great teacher.

Possessing knowledge and skill is one thing, but being able to impart that knowledge and skill to a student is another. Jimmy was the best of both worlds and was all around one of the nicest persons we have met. Before we knew it, Sharon finished her training, took her checkride, and had earned her license. She was officially a pilot!

It was truly an interesting time for both of us. Sharon was learning to fly while, at the same time, her oldest of two sons was learning to drive. I had my hands full, to say the least, as I was actively involved with both training missions.

In the meantime, I had also flown with Jimmy and was busy jumping through hoops to satisfy the FAA. I had to acquire a waiver because of my medical condition as one uses their feet to operate the rudder pedals and the brakes. I was also going to have to fly with an inspector from the FAA for what was called a "609" (something to do with the regulation number) checkride to get my license reinstated. I really had no idea what was in store since nobody I knew had ever dealt with the situation I was in, and nobody at the FAA office could give me a definitive answer. So I just studied and practiced so that I would be able to answer any question or do any maneuver that was thrown at me on the ride.

It actually was not as difficult a process as I first thought that it might be. On November 17, 1994, I met with an inspector from the FAA at Northeast

Philadelphia Airport. Since I could not legally fly by myself yet, I rented Jimmy for the afternoon and took him with me. I couldn't have picked a worse day; it was very windy because of a front moving in. And to top it off, the inspector, who I'll call Joe, was roughly an hour and a half late. And the later it got, the windier it got.

So Joe showed up, introduced himself, and said, "So just what is it that we are supposed to be doing today?" I was really hoping that he would have known what to do since nobody else did.

"I have absolutely no idea," I replied, all the while saying under my breath, "Your boss said that you're just supposed to sign me off. He knows that I know what I'm doing."

But I figured that such a statement might come back to bite me, so I kept mute and then simply asked if we could review the areas in which I had difficulty.

He ended up asking me some questions about my accident and reviewing some material, and then we went flying. But by that point, the winds were in excess of thirty knots and were gusting, so it was not a fun ride. But we went up, stalled the plane a few times to make sure I recovered properly, and did a few takeoffs and landings, and he was satisfied. Despite the uncertainty in the beginning, it ended up being a productive afternoon. He signed my paperwork, and my license was officially reinstated. It was a momentous day for me. Despite having limitations as to what types of aircraft I would be allowed to fly due to my legs not working 100%, I had proven to myself that I could do it.

Sharon and I enjoyed any time spent flying, but most important was any time spent together. We were best friends and soul mates, and I knew that I needed to marry her, that I needed her in my life forever. On Valentine's Day 1996, I asked Sharon to marry me while we were up in a plane flying through a most beautiful sky. The moon and the stars were picture perfect. Sharon always gets a little mushy when she tells this story, but I just tell people that it was a wonderful night, a picture-perfect flight. And best of all, she said she would marry me.

Everyone should take the opportunity to go flying at night at least once in their life. And I mean in a small plane, not on an airliner. There is something that is so beautiful and serene about being in an airplane at night with the sky full of stars and a full moon. The way that a full moon illuminates the ground and makes it glow is simply amazing and has to be experienced in order to be appreciated. All right, so I get a little mushy too. What can I say? Although time doesn't always allow as many opportunities as before, an occasional flight through a beautiful nighttime sky gives us the chance to relive an event that will always be special in our hearts.

We both had a great deal of fun planning our wedding. I've heard so many people talk about the stress of planning a wedding, but, to be truthful, I've never understood that. It was actually a smooth process even down to the smallest of details, and I really had an absolute blast doing it. We were married on September 28, 1996, with approximately a hundred friends and family members. We had a big church wedding and a wonderful reception following the ceremony. Sharon's two sons walked her down the aisle and gave her away, as her father had passed away quite a few years ago. She looked radiant as she approached the altar, and it was a day that will always be special in my heart.

Sharon and I spent a week in Nashville for our honeymoon and had a wonderful time.

I was in great hands during the flights to and from Nashville, as Sharon was doing the flying. We decided to fly into Nashville International instead of one of the smaller airports in the boondocks. There is nothing like being lined up for approach at night in a small plane, following an airliner, with a few more lined up on approach behind you. I love it!

We went to the Grand Ole Opry as well as many other sights and saw many of the country-music stars. Nashville is a really nice place to go whether you like country music or not. Of course, we have a little joke whenever someone tells us that they don't like country music. We just tell them that admitting the problem is the first step! Following our honeymoon, we quickly got settled into our new house: a rancher, thank goodness. Although I was slightly better than I had been a few years prior, I really preferred to not have to deal with stairs. In addition to her duties as director of the day care center, Sharon had begun a floral-design business on the side. Her work is magnificent, and she enjoys it very much. Given our love for music, we had started a disc jockey business, and I was also doing some live shows singing country music. I was performing at some local bars and restaurants as well as some festivals and street fairs. We were having fun, and life was going along just fine, which led me to make the mistake of becoming complacent. I didn't believe that anything could stop us at this point.

Sharon's First Scare

In early 2002 Sharon needed to have some minor foot surgery, which was to be a simple procedure. While going through the requisite poking and prodding of the preadmission testing, the physician's assistant kept focusing on her neck and listening with his stethoscope. He was hearing a noise called a *bruit* (pronounced brew-ee). It is sort of a "whooshing" sound with each heartbeat. Think of how the sound changes when you kink a garden hose and the water can't get through. It's similar to that but cycles with each heartbeat. He explained that this is something seen primarily in older people, and that given Sharon's age, it probably wasn't a big deal. He added that it might be worth talking to our doctor about, but definitely she didn't need to worry.

Being one that likes to have all of the bases covered, I have learned that the one time that we definitely need to worry is when someone is telling us that they are certain that there is nothing to worry about. I'm just kind of funny that way.

The foot surgery went as expected, which is to say that it was a non-event. Sharon spent a few weeks in a surgical boot while keeping weight off of the foot, and she was better than new in no time. Except that the *bruit* was weighing heavily on our minds. We went

to visit our primary care physician that we were seeing at the time. He really didn't seem too worried and
explained that this type of thing is really only a problem that is seen in much older people. I had done some
research on this, and while it true that it is generally
seen in older people, it is indicative of build-up and
clogging in the arteries. Despite the doctor's efforts to
convince us that a person in their forties didn't need to
worry, we were not about to let this go.

I explained to the doctor that Sharon's father
had passed away at fifty-six years old due to coro-
nary issues. There was a family history of high cholesterol that was not diet related, and Sharon was
taking medication to control hers. Nana (her father's
mother), on the other hand, had the same issues as
well as diabetes and lived past ninety because she had
taken a very proactive and aggressive approach to her
health care. We were sticking with Nana's plan.

So the question for the doctor was, if Sharon was
of the age group where this might be a concern, what
test would he order? He wrote the order for an ultrasound of the carotid arteries, still confident that this
wasn't going to be a big deal.

Needless to say, the ultrasound confirmed what
I believed to be the case. The test indicated that the
right carotid artery was 50% blocked and the left was
70% blocked. We were referred to a vascular surgeon,
who wanted to do a few more tests that would be a
little more accurate than the ultrasound.

It didn't surprise me when, at our next meeting
with the surgeon, the first thing he did was open up

his calendar. That's usually the first clue that he's looking for a date to schedule surgery. That isn't to say that we didn't see it coming. The MRI had shown more blockage than originally thought, so we were fully aware that surgery would be necessary. The surgeon was not planning anything for the right side, as the blockage was not as bad. Given the risks of this type of surgery, there is no way they will go in for a vessel that is only 50% to 60% blocked. The left side was another story. They would have to go into Sharon's neck, open up the artery, and clear it out. I won't go so far as to say that we weren't afraid or concerned, but neither of us is the type that generally comes unglued and falls apart when dealing with medical matters. We both have been cut enough times that we are used to it. Our attitude was more along the lines of, *what needs to be done? What is involved? What day do we need to show up?* Sure, we realized the complexity of the procedure and the seriousness of it, but there was no other option. We weren't about to ignore it, as problems don't usually get better on their own, and we had the utmost confidence in the vascular surgeon who would be performing the procedure.

We arrived on the appointed day, and the team began to get Sharon ready for her surgery. The first thing they did was attach many wires to her head that would allow them to monitor brain activity during the surgery through an electroencephalogram (EEG). Due to the complexity of the surgery, one of the possible risks is that the patient could suffer a stroke, thus the need for the EEG. The vast array of wires on Sharon's head was a most attractive sight, and we considered wheeling her across the street and going through the shopping mall to see if we could start a new fashion trend. I was betting that if we did, within several days we would see lots of teenagers walking around with wires in their hair.

I think the operating room staff thought we were just a little crazy; there's nothing like a little humor or sarcasm to break the tension! We were just slightly nervous. I spoke to the surgeon before he went in to the operating room and asked him to please have the best day he has ever had. And I prayed to God to bless the surgeon and to watch over Sharon throughout this ordeal.

The surgery went well, and I met with the doctor immediately following. It turned out that the tests had been off a little bit and that the left carotid artery had been 99% blocked off. Sharon was a candidate for a stroke, and we didn't even know it. Sharon and I felt a flood of emotions as a result of this news—fear over just how close she came to a stroke, frustration that the one doctor had downplayed the issue, and relief that the problem was corrected in time. We also felt a sense of gratitude to the vascular surgeon, as well as the person who notified us of the problem in the first place. If the physician's assistant doing the preadmission testing hadn't heard the *bruit* or hadn't alerted us to it, Sharon might have died. Chalk one up for the good guys! Once again, God had been watching over us; however, we walked away from this with a valuable lesson. And the lesson is that it is vitally important to take an active role in one's own care. Trust what your gut tells you.

Sharon remained in the intensive care unit overnight so she could be closely monitored and came home shortly thereafter. It didn't take long for Sharon to be back to her normal schedule, but the surgeon said that she should have ultrasounds performed on her neck annually just to keep an eye on everything.

By 2004 an ultrasound showed questionable lymph nodes in Sharon's neck. Both lymph nodes were removed and sent out for biopsy in two separate procedures, and fortunately, both were benign. And fortunately, we both have a sense of humor. When a person has as many scars as we both do, it's important to make up some good stories to go with them.

Right after the surgery to remove the second lymph node, I had received a phone call from a lady that owned a local restaurant and bar, who was looking for some musical entertainment, country and western in particular. I had previously dropped off one of my demo discs, so she had already had the chance to hear me sing. I stopped down to see her, and we agreed on the terms, at which point she began telling me about all of her "rules" that she expected everyone to abide by, such as not tolerating drunks or fighting or any such bad behavior. She was running a respectable place. Apparently, it was the standard speech that she gave everyone who came through the door to entertain there.

I had forgotten to share this little bit of the story with Sharon. Well, the night I went to sing there, Sharon was with me, as always (she worked the sound board) but was sporting a very large bandage on her neck from the surgery. I introduced her to the owner of the establishment, who inquired about the large bandage. What did Sharon respond with? "Oh, I can't seem to stay out of bar fights," she said! We almost got fired before we got started. I can't take her anywhere!

One of the many things that I adore about Sharon is her sense of humor and spontaneity. I never know what to expect from her, and I recall once telling her back when we were still courting that I knew life with her would never be boring. She has certainly stepped up and met the challenge head on. She is one funny lady. Sharon mended quickly, and we were even allowed to go back to that restaurant again.

Life got back to normal, and we put the past behind us. We continued to thank God for His blessings and continued to watch Sharon's health, although it appeared that we were out of the woods. As long as we kept an eye on her cholesterol and blood pressure, life would be fine. And once again, I took life for granted. This, however, would be the last time.

Sharon and Guillain-Barré Syndrome

Sharon continued to do well with her floral arrangements and in the spring of 2006 was gearing up for what would hopefully be a good year. Sharon participated in various floral and craft shows, and the schedule for the year was looking promising. Sharon had been in the hospital again in March for an outpatient procedure to remove a cyst from her right maxillary sinus; however, it wasn't a big deal. We had recently been in Florida for a short spell and were relaxed and ready to go. Life was good. The road that we were traveling was nothing but smooth, straight highways.

On Thursday, April 27, 2006, we had been in the Baltimore area for a show, and it had been a long day. That evening when we got home, Sharon mentioned that she felt a little funny. She said that her fingertips felt like pins and needles and that her feet felt as if she were "walking on wet sponges." I was crystal clear on the pins and needles, as what few parts of my legs and feet that I can feel have similar sensations. But walking on wet sponges? That was a new one on me, and I really didn't know what to make of it at first. Sharon normally takes a diuretic but had not taken it that day. Nothing else had been different in her routine.

The following day Sharon wasn't feeling any better, and she was able to get an appointment with the doctor for that afternoon. A pinched nerve was suspected, and X-rays of the cervical spine were ordered to see if that would show anything. I had some initial concerns since the problem was affecting both upper and lower extremities bilaterally but decided to wait and see what the X-rays would show. But I was still somewhat skeptical.

Given that it was late on a Friday, X-rays were going to have to wait until the following week. Saturday afternoon we attended a family gathering, and Sharon was her typical cheery self, although the odd sensations in her hands and feet persisted. By the time we arrived home that evening, Sharon was experiencing difficulty performing even the simplest of tasks with her hands and told me that the sensation in her feet had turned to numbness and had crept up as far as her ankles. In a matter of minutes, we were at the emergency room.

The emergency room team ran a series of tests and told us that Sharon's potassium level was low. Actually, we already knew that, as that had shown up during preadmission testing for her sinus surgery almost two months prior. But obviously it wasn't of grave concern since the surgery was performed with that knowledge. I was just having an extremely difficult time believing that her symptoms were being caused by low potassium. And then the light clicked on in my head, and I expressed my concern to the emergency room doctor. I told him that I suspected that we could possibly be looking at a case of Guillain-Barré Syndrome (GBS) and asked if it was possible to at least rule it out. GBS is a rare illness that results in the immune system attacking one's own body and basically destroying the nervous system, causing muscle weakness in mild cases and paralysis in severe cases. I had previously witnessed the effects of GBS, as a friend was stricken with this illness years ago, and the results of GBS are not always pretty. But needless to say, I was looked at as if I had horns sprouting out of my head. Who was I to tell them anything? They were sticking to the potassium theory and decided to admit Sharon and keep her overnight. I stayed with Sharon in her hospital room until roughly four a.m. I went home, took a short nap, and then prepared to come back to the hospital.

I was back in Sharon's hospital room by eight thirty Sunday morning. She was weaker than the night before and now required assistance to walk to the bathroom. I even had to hold a cup of water for her in order for her to take a drink. In my humble opinion, this still did not look like the results of low potassium. In addition, Sharon was experiencing intense pain across her lower back.

It wasn't long before the doctors were making rounds, and we spoke at length regarding Sharon's case and specifically my suspicions regarding GBS. We discussed the disease in great depth, and he wrote orders for her to be seen by both a nephrologist and a neurologist. The nephrologist examined Sharon and determined that there was nothing wrong regarding the kidneys that could have been causing the intense pain in her back. This made sense, as it would be highly unlikely that something would affect both kidneys simultaneously and cause so much pain across the entire back. I thanked him for his time and waited patiently for the neurologist. And waited.

In between tending to Sharon's needs, I began making phone calls to update family members. I also called Patty Benson, who is Sharon's assistant at the day care center. I let Patty know of Sharon's status and that she would not be in on Monday. Deep down inside I had a feeling that it would be a long time past Monday before she would see Sharon at work again. But I just couldn't have that discussion at that point.

The nursing staff continued to administer potassium through Sharon's intravenous line.

They were sticking to the belief that if they gave Sharon enough potassium, it would solve the problem. By mid-afternoon, Sharon was weaker and had minimal mobility in her arms and legs, and we still had not seen a neurologist.

Sharon's sister Ann arrived, and we began to try to figure out the best way to handle this. And by now, all of the fluid that was being administered was taking its toll on Sharon. After all, what goes in must come out. By now she could no longer walk, so Ann and I had to assist her with this little "mission." Unfortunately, her bladder was one of the muscles now affected, and as a result, she could not void. Sharon was in extreme discomfort, and I informed the nurse and asked for a catheter kit.

The nurse seemed a little dumbfounded about my request. I told the nurse that either she was going to do the procedure or I was, but I wanted Sharon out of her state of discomfort. After all of the time I had spent in the spinal cord injury unit, I was quite familiar with the process of catheterization and was up to the task of doing it. However, the nurse went and retrieved a kit, and it was taken care of in short order.

It was going on five in the afternoon when I went to the nurses' station and inquired about the neurologist, as nobody had shown up yet. The nurse responded by saying that if we hadn't seen anybody yet, then we probably wouldn't see them until the next day, given the time of day at that point. Not being satisfied with that answer, I asked her to please put a call in and find out. Once again I was assured that as soon as Sharon's potassium level was back to normal, she would be fine.

We waited patiently, and Ann and I discussed the idea of transferring Sharon to a different hospital. It wasn't long before Sharon started to decline quickly. Her body was limp. The muscles on the right side of her face were no longer functioning. I had to put my ear next to her to hear what she was saying, and she was going into respiratory arrest. The nerves that controlled her diaphragm had been compromised, and now we were losing her.

I quickly made my way once again to the nurses' station and told them they needed to move *now!* It was just prior to seven p.m., and Sharon's nurse was in the process of giving report to the oncoming shift. Ann and I were both horrified when one of the nurses responded by saying that they didn't know what to do. This was beginning to feel like a really bad dream. I just couldn't believe that this was happening. Everybody seemed to be running in slow motion, and I told the nurse that she needed to "call a code." She obliged, and I heard the call go out over the public address system as I made my way back to be with Sharon.

Suddenly I saw a flood of people coming down the hall pushing all kinds of equipment. They began connecting various machines and monitors to Sharon. Sharon could barely take a breath by this point, and her facial muscles had gotten so weak that her eyes were no longer tracking together. I can truly say that I have never witnessed such a state of panic. The look of fear on the faces of the staff can't be described, and I couldn't even begin to imagine what Sharon was thinking at that point.

Imagine being on an airliner flying through stormy conditions and hearing screaming come from the cockpit. It wouldn't instill much confidence, would it? Well, that is about how we felt at this point. We were now fearful. These people were professionals, and they looked scared and couldn't hide it. It would be months before Sharon would be able to tell me her side of this experience. In fact, it would be months before Sharon would be able to tell me anything. But she too recalls the look of fear and horror on the faces of the doctors. She later told me that it was at that point she knew that it was going to be a long time before she would be coming home. This was serious, and Sharon knew it.

One of the doctors was about to perform an ultrasound when the neurologist we had been waiting all day for was suddenly available to examine Sharon. How sporting of her. She did a brief exam on Sharon, tapped a few joints with a hammer to test reflexes, and inquired if Sharon's eyes "always looked like that." She was referring to the fact that Sharon's eyes were now pointing in different directions, as the facial muscles on the right side had now been affected. The disease was traveling quickly. Sharon later told me that what was going through her mind was, *Oh, great, my eyes too, just what I need!*

What happened next I will never forget. The neurologist turned to the doctor with the ultrasound machine and said, as coldly as could be, "Your machine's not going to tell you anything I don't already know. This is Guillain-Barré Syndrome." My heart sank, and I must confess that the next few words out of my mouth would not have won me a congeniality award. The neurologist then said to me, "This is not a big deal, and it is very treatable." I did not believe a word of it. I do not think that it would have been possible for that doctor to have cared any less.

After more time passed than I was comfortable with, the team began to intubate Sharon, as she was no longer able to breathe at all on her own, and she was connected to a ventilator. It would turn out that there was a lapse of approximately forty-five minutes that Sharon was in respiratory distress, a timeline that was confirmed by information in the medical records. I was not happy with these folks.

I moved the conversation outside of the room only to have the neurologist seem bewildered and ask me why I was so upset, insisting that this illness was not a big deal. To this day I will never understand why she said what she did. The attitude that she displayed was just not anything we were accustomed to. I told her that I had seen GBS before and that I was very aware of what was ahead. The fact is, so did Sharon. She has met the man that I know from my fire and ambulance days who had been stricken with GBS years ago, so she too had seen the results of it. My heart was broken, as now Sharon had a complete understanding of what was in her future.

There was one particular gal that we knew from anesthesiology who happened to be working that night. She came out of the room in tears when she realized that it was Sharon who was in distress. I had been really hoping that somebody besides Ann and I would have been able to keep it together.

I looked at Ann, who looked at me, and our eyes said all that needed to be said; it was time to leave. Sharon needed to be downtown at Jefferson. The neurologist mentioned the idea of doing a spinal tap, which is one of the tests for GBS. I declined on that idea, as I knew that it would be done once we got downtown, and I didn't want to subject Sharon to it twice. And I didn't want her laying another hand on my wife. Enough damage had been done.

It felt as if our world was crumbling. While I prayed that she would survive, I was afraid of what was in the future for Sharon. Paralysis is an awful thing; I remembered what I went through, except I hadn't been on a ventilator. Sharon was moved to the intensive care unit to be monitored while arrangements were made to transport her. I don't know how to find the words to describe the feelings that were going through me, but for the first time I had a basic understanding of what my family went through when I had been in the airplane accident in 1990. I believe that watching a loved one cling to life is about as bad as it can get. All of the emotions I had struggled with after my accident could not compare in any way to what I felt that night.

I could see the fear in Sharon's eyes. At this point all that she was able to do was see and hear; she was totally paralyzed, relying on a machine for her every breath. I remained by her side and did my best to comfort and assure her that she would get through this, all the while trying not to look as though I was as afraid as I was. I've never had a very good "poker face," and Sharon later told me that she could see the fear in everyone's eyes, including mine. So if you ever see me break out a deck of cards, you probably don't want to be my partner! Not to say that I'm bad under pressure; I just can't always hide it.

It did not help Sharon to overhear the one doctor

saying to me repeatedly, "I'm so sorry that we missed this." Yeah, we were kind of sorry too. What kept racing through my mind is that we had discussed GBS that morning during rounds. This doctor talked about how one of his sons had been stricken with this disease. How did he not see this? I felt as if we had been betrayed.

———————

As the time passed, I made several phone calls to let folks know what was happening while I was waiting for the helicopter. I called Patty again to give her an update and let her know that Sharon was now on life support and that she needed to just keep business as usual at the day care center. I was very clear that she was to tell nobody about what was happening.

Bad news has a way of causing panic, and I envisioned two possible scenarios, the first being that people might wonder if the center would close as a result of Sharon's condition and start making other arrangements for child care. That definitely would have closed the center if all of the clients had pulled out.

The second scenario I envisioned is that although GBS is not contagious, most people have never heard of it and would not know that. So it was possible that clients could panic, think that it is, and fear that their child was exposed to something. There was nothing to worry about with either regard, so I felt it was best for the time being to run things as normally as possible. Yes, people would notice that Sharon wasn't there, but I would deal with that when it became necessary. I now had a day care center in my lap as well and would learn more in the next five months than I ever wanted to know.

Ann stayed with me for a while, but then she and a few family members left to go into the city to wait for Sharon to arrive. I wanted to stay with Sharon until it was time to leave, but I wanted Ann to be downtown when Sharon arrived there. I asked one of the nurses who was in contact with the staff at Jefferson to let me know the instant the helicopter was airborne.

Shortly before midnight, the nurse came in to tell me that they had gotten the call and that the helicopter had just lifted off of the pad at Jefferson. I said another prayer, hugged and kissed Sharon, and told her good-bye and that I would see her downtown.

Another Trip Downtown

Having lost the ability to run many years ago, it took a bit of time to get from the intensive care unit down to the parking lot. As I was driving away, it kept running through my mind that all of this couldn't possibly be happening. I kept waiting to wake up from this awful dream. So much for life being a smooth, straight highway—we had definitely hit the twist in the road.

I had only gone a few miles when I saw the lights from the helicopter overhead on its way to pick up Sharon, and I pushed the accelerator harder. I needed to get to Philadelphia before the helicopter, as I had told Sharon that I would be there when she arrived. Fortunately, the police were not patrolling the interstate that night. I think I may have broken a speed limit or two—dozen. As I pulled into the parking garage at Jefferson Hospital, I heard a familiar thunderous noise overhead. I wasn't going to make it in time, as that was the helicopter approaching the landing pad on the roof. I had beaten them, but they would have the advantage over me on foot.

By the time I made my way to the ninth floor, Sharon had already been taken into a room in the neurosensory intensive care unit (NICU). This was like déjà vu all over again, except that the last time

I had been there, I was the one that had arrived by helicopter and come in through the roof. Sharon's family was there, and I was glad that she was able to see them as she was wheeled past. She later would describe their faces as ashen gray in color. She could see in their eyes that they were scared to death that she was going to die. She had no way to reach out and reassure them, and she has told me that even at that moment, she knew she could survive all of this.

Once Sharon was transferred into a bed and stabilized, I was allowed back to see her. Naturally, all of her family wanted the chance to see her, but it was impossible to accommodate them. The staff was very strict about only allowing one person back at this point, as they had to get working on Sharon. I asked them to bend the rule and allow Ann to come back to the room, as I wanted her there for any conversation with the doctors.

Ann and I were to spend the next five months working together to take care of all of Sharon's needs. It would turn out that I could not have asked for a better teammate, as her input and assistance would prove to be invaluable.

We met with one of the doctors, who had been well briefed on Sharon's case prior to her arrival. Fortunately, I was in a position to speak intelligently regarding Sharon's medical history, as I have always insisted that we go to all doctor visits together when possible. After a brief but thorough conversation with the doctors, it was time for us to leave. They were getting Sharon ready for the spinal tap as well as a CAT scan and certainly didn't need us in the way. And it's not as if we could be of any help.

While we were all sure that this was GBS, there's nothing like an ounce of prevention.

They just wanted to rule out any secondary neurological issues, such as a stroke, so I was 100% in favor of the CAT scan. While it is protocol to get permission to perform any test or procedure, I told them to simply do whatever they had to do to keep her alive. If something came up, and it was life or death, don't call me; save Sharon. They told me to call in a few hours for an update.

It was somewhere around three thirty a.m. Monday, May 1; I was on my way home, and Ann headed back to her home in New Jersey. My mind was on overload. Sharon was paralyzed and on life support, and while GBS in and of itself is not fatal, complications could prove otherwise. I was facing a very bitter reality that Sharon could possibly die. They say that it is always darkest before dawn; how true—things couldn't get much darker. The beautiful woman who is the love of my life was hanging on to life by a thread. I got home and all I could do was pray. I asked God to please spare Sharon from this ordeal. If I could have taken her place, I would have in an instant.

I didn't sleep during what was left of the night but spent a lot of time asking God to give us the wisdom, strength, and courage to face what was ahead of us. I mostly needed the wisdom, as I now had a full plate in front of me, and was going to have to be making many decisions on things that I knew little about. In addition to everything going on with Sharon and life in general, I was determined to keep the day care center viable. It had been around for several decades and wasn't going to fall on my watch. Needless to say, I had a lot on my mind.

By six a.m. I was on the phone to the NICU at Jefferson and spoke with one of the doctors. Everything had gone well with the tests, with the spinal tap confirming the GBS and the CAT scan of the brain ruling out anything else neurological. After tending to a few things at the day care center that morning, I headed back downtown to the hospital.

The agenda for the day was to include the first of five treatments known as plasmapheresis, which is the technical term for plasma replacement. Basically, the blood is removed from the body in a manner similar to someone being on dialysis, but instead of being filtered, it is run through a centrifuge where the blood cells and the plasma are separated. The plasma that has the bad antibodies in it is discarded, and then the blood cells are mixed with new plasma and returned to the body. This procedure would be performed five times over the next ten days to thoroughly flush out her body.

Later that day, Ann and I discussed Sharon's case at length and began to formulate a "game plan" to ensure a successful recovery. I believe firmly that there is little chance of success in anything without a plan of action. While it is true that we had Sharon at what is probably the best hospital that there is for neurological issues, there was still a lot that we could and needed to do. Sharon was facing several issues as a result of being sedentary and hospitalized, and while we had faith in the staff, I felt that it was very necessary to be proactive and remain involved.

The first issue Sharon would face would be the risk of infections. The fact is, hospitals are full of sick people, and the potential for the spreading of those germs is very great. In addition, every visitor that walks through the door is carrying germs. I posted a sign in Sharon's room as well as issued verbal reminders to everybody regarding washing their hands upon entering her room.

In fact, the sign actually read:

> *Everybody* wash your hands. If you don't,
> and you give my sweetheart germs and make
> her sick, I'll kick your butt! Love, Bob

The "Love, Bob" thing was part of the soft side of me that I so rarely show. I quickly became everybody's worst nightmare on the topic of hand washing and the prevention of infection. But it is a necessary precaution for everyone when near a patient.

My second area of concern was that of maintaining Sharon's skin condition. Many people have heard of bed sores but are not familiar with them. People are at risk when they are immobile for long periods of time, as I had explained when describing my time in the body cast. I find it appalling that this still happens from time to time. Fortunately, the staff in the NICU was just as aggressive about skin care as the staff had been with me in 1990 and turned Sharon consistently to keep her skin in good order.

However, Ann and I decided that it would be a good idea for us to inspect her skin daily. As Ronald Reagan once said, "Trust, but verify." In the time that I had spent in my body cast, I was taught very early on the importance of weight shifting to protect skin integrity. I would apply this same regiment to Sharon's care.

Thirdly, I was concerned about Sharon's muscles and the effects that atrophy would have on her body. When muscles aren't used, they basically waste away. In addition, muscles and tendons will begin to tighten up from lack of use. Ann and I began a routine of doing passive range of motion exercises on Sharon. That's a nice way of saying we stretched her! Granted, the hospital therapy staff would be doing this; however, there is no such thing as too much attention to this matter. When the body is dormant, atrophy is one of the hardest battles to fight, so we kept at it daily.

Finally, we also included in our plan that one or both of us needed to be there every day. I am not saying that I didn't have confidence in the staff, but the truth is, there's nothing like being there in person to monitor what is going on. And there's nothing like being there in person to let Sharon know that we were a team and that we would get through this. I knew that she needed me there.

So Ann and I had our plan set up, and we just needed to carry it through. We talked or met every day and remained committed to making sure that Sharon was taken care of. And within a few days, it seemed that Sharon was making progress.

The only way in which Sharon could communicate was to ask her questions and have her blink her eyes: once for yes and twice for no. This made communication rather cumbersome, as it often involved a lot of questions and a lot of blinking.

One evening I could tell that she needed something, so I ran through the list of questions and waited for the appropriate response:

Need the nurse?	2 blinks
Need to be suctioned?	2 blinks
Water?	2 blinks
Ice pack?	2 blinks
Turn over?	2 blinks
Kisses?	1 blink

Yeehah! Kisses! But I must admit that it was tough with that airway tube in the way!

Unfortunately, we had to take Sharon's wedding ring off that night due to excessive swelling. It required a bit of effort, but I wanted to get it off before we had to cut it off. It turned out that Sharon's wedding ring fit my pinky finger just right, so I wore it on my left pinky next to my wedding ring for the duration of her hospital stay. It was my way of having her next to me all of the time even though we couldn't be together constantly.

And so, in my own little silly mind, I came up

with an idea for one of those sappy credit card commercials. I still might send the suggestion in to them; we'll see!

* Intensive-care hospital room–$2,500.00 per day

* Helicopter transport to Jefferson–$10,000.00

* Your wife wanting kisses, and you wearing her wedding ring next to yours–*Priceless!*

Well, maybe I don't have a future in advertising after all.

It didn't take long for Sharon to get tired of having the airway tube down her throat. She had no way to call the nurse if she needed to, since she could not actuate a typical call button, but figured out that if she bit down on the airway tube, it would restrict airflow and trigger the alarm, indicating a problem with the ventilator. Simple, but it was effective.

On Friday, May 5, the doctors removed the airway tube, put a small incision in her neck, and inserted the tracheotomy tube. This was a great relief as Sharon had actually been looking forward to the procedure. Despite the fact that it meant cutting a hole in her neck, she was rid of the discomfort of having the large airway tube in her mouth and down her throat. This, of course, left her with no way to call a nurse. One of the occupational therapists came up with a large switch for Sharon and clipped it to the pillow right next to her cheek (not those cheeks, the cheek on her face, silly!). Sharon had just enough strength in her neck to allow her to turn her head and hit the switch if she needed help.

On the same day, the doctors also cut a small hole

to insert the feeding tube into her stomach, enabling Sharon to receive nutrition. It's a really good thing that they feed you through the tube directly to the stomach, as I can't imagine swallowing the stuff. It smelled terrible!

As much as I'm not a real computer guy, I found that the most effective way to update everyone on Sharon's progress was by way of e-mail. There were times that I was often up for several days straight, and taking the time to call people to update them just was not an option. I set up a group list to which I gave the title *Prayer Warriors* and would send out constant updates to all of those who were constantly bending God's ear. I'm sure at some point, God figured Sharon had better get well, or he would never stop hearing her name. We had a prayer chain that spread from as far south as Florida, as far north as Canada, and across the country all the way out west to Washington.

Sharon has a long-time friend who is a Latin teacher. I called Martha at school to let her know about Sharon. Her first words when she got on the phone were, "What's wrong with Sharon?" It was obvious I would not have called her at school just to chat. Martha has been a friend not only to Sharon but to the day care center as well and was devastated to hear the news.

Being Martha, she offered to help in any way she could, and I knew that she meant it.

I assured her that I would be calling her, as I was definitely in over my head. I had been praying for help with managing the affairs at the day care center, especially cash flow. A few days later, a friend of Martha's dropped off a three-thousand-dollar donation. Nobody will ever successfully convince me that prayers don't work!

Later that same day, the doctors told us that someone from the cast room would be up to make splints for Sharon's wrists to help support them while she was immobile. And of all people to show up, it was Tony, who had put my body cast on me sixteen years prior!

I looked at him and said, "I know you!" Without even hesitating, Tony said, "You were Doctor Cotler's patient; I put that orange body cast on you!" I couldn't believe that he remembered. As he approached me, I extended my hand to shake his; however, he went right past it and went straight for a hug. It was great to see a familiar face and to know that he was involved in Sharon's care. He didn't press me for any donations this time though, as he didn't have his cast saw with him!

Sharon was also fitted with a set of special ankle supports to keep her feet from dropping, as that is common when patients are immobile for long periods of time. In addition, she also had to wear a set of inflatable boots to keep the blood circulating in her legs. Blood clots are a persistent threat, and these boots inflate at preset intervals to squeeze the legs and keep the blood moving. I had to wear them when I was in the hospital and couldn't stand them, and Sharon's sentiments were quite similar.

Within a week Sharon seemed to be improving somewhat, but this would prove to be for a short duration before things would worsen. I knew I had to keep my faith, but I must admit that it was difficult. Sharon had come down with pneumonia as well as a secondary respiratory infection. This is not uncommon with ventilator patients, but knowing that really didn't make it any easier to deal with.

Sharon was fighting so hard, but there was nothing anyone could do except let this illness run its course. Sharon had received all of her plasmapheresis treatments, but that does not undo the nerve damage. The plasmapheresis simply got rid of all of the bad antibodies that had destroyed Sharon's nerves.

Nerves do regenerate, but only at a rate of approximately one millimeter per day. As a point of reference, there are, in round numbers, twenty-five millimeters per inch. I never did like that metric system stuff. Needless to say, recovery was going to take a long time, as most of the nerves in Sharon's body had been affected in some way.

In many cases of GBS, only the myelin sheath is affected. Think of that as insulation on a wire. Those cases are generally not as severe. But Sharon also had axonal damage, meaning that the nerve itself was compromised as well. Yep, that's my Sharon, my little overachiever. Axonal damage, plus the Fisher variation of GBS that affects the facial muscles, and being on the ventilator—she went all the way on this one.

Sharon and I worked to overcome our struggle with communication, as it involved asking a multitude of questions until she blinked once indicating that I had guessed correctly. We were both growing tired of this, so I switched to a new program. I brought in one of those small erasable marker boards and put the alphabet on it, broken up into four blocks. This way Sharon could pick out letters by blinking when I pointed to them, and we could actually make sentences. It allowed us to move a little bit quicker; pick a block and then pick a letter in that block. This eased a lot of frustration, and now Sharon was able to convey her thoughts a little more clearly.

In addition, I set up a large marker board on an easel in Sharon's room with any and all pertinent information listed that I felt was necessary. With that arrangement, anybody who walked into that room could instantly see vital information that I wanted known before even looking at her chart.

———————

By the time we were going into the third week, Sharon's condition had reached an all-time low. She had an infection in her blood, she was still totally dependent on the ventilator, her hemoglobin level was at the point that required her to have blood transfusions, and she could no longer blink her eyes. This just was not going well. Her blood vessels were at a point where it was almost impossible to keep a line going, so they started a line under the clavicle. That worked a little better, as they were able to hit a blood vessel that was bigger than those in Sharon's arms.

We had to put drops and ointment in her eyes to keep them from drying out, and we alternated putting a patch on her eyes every two hours; first one eye and then the other so at least she could see a little bit. I was devastated by all of this, mostly because of knowing how it must have been affecting Sharon. She hated having that goopy crap put into her eyes as it made everything cloudy, but there was no option.

I had serious doubts as to whether she was going to make it through all of this. I recall praying to God and asking, "Lord, if you are going to take her, then please take her and ease her suffering, but if it is your will that she will be healed, please heal her quickly and give her the strength to fight." I felt somewhat guilty asking God in such a way, but it was so difficult to watch her go through all of this.

Just when things seemed to be at their lowest point, two people sent cards, both of which had one of my favorite verses on it. The verse is called "Footprints." It goes as follows:

Footprints

One night a man had a dream about walking along the beach with the Lord. The sky flashed scenes from his life. For each scene, he noticed two sets of footprints in the sand: his and the Lord's.

After the last scene flashed before him, he looked at the footprints, noticing that at the most difficult times in his life there was only one set of footprints.

"Lord, you said you'd walk with me all the way if I followed you. But during the most troublesome times in my life, there is only one set of footprints. Why did you leave me when I needed you most?"

The Lord replied, "I love you and would never leave you. In your times of trial and suffering, when you see only one set of footprints, that was when I carried you." (Author Unknown)

Fortunately, my prayers were answered for the better. Sharon's condition stabilized, and on May 22, she was transferred to the step-down unit but then had an encounter with a blood clot in her trachea. We had gone two steps forward and then one step back. The staff took care of the problem quickly, and Sharon was out of danger once again but extremely fatigued.

It would be several months before Sharon could talk and tell me her side of the experience. An important thing to understand here is that Sharon was conscious and totally aware of what was going on throughout her entire hospitalization. Two doctors were working on her trying to get the blood clot, and they initially were not having total success. She heard one doctor say several times that he "couldn't get the blood clot; the machine just wasn't strong enough." The thought that was running through her mind was, *For crying out loud, this is Jefferson Hospital! Just go get a bigger machine; I'm sure you have one!*

The next words from one doctor to the other were, "I think I'm going to get the bigger machine." Hallelujah! Either it was a case of divine intervention, or the doctor was psychic. Either way, it worked out, and we can laugh about it now. There was no laughter that day, however.

The most amazing thing about all of this is that no matter how bad things got, Sharon's attitude stayed positive all of the time. That's not to say that she wasn't scared at times, but she had made the conscious decision to fight and win. She later told me that the night she was flown in the helicopter, she had made that decision. As she was being loaded into the helicopter, all she could do at that point was see and hear. She told herself that the only thing left that she had control over was her attitude, and nobody was going to take it away! She carried that mindset for the duration of her illness and continues to do so to this day.

I was soon informed that I was going to have to start making arrangements to transfer Sharon to another facility. There was really nothing else that could be done for Sharon at this point, but as we know, insurance companies dictate what goes on. And those that were calling the shots were saying that the time was quickly approaching when Sharon would have to leave, as she no longer needed to be in intensive care. I was a little uncertain, as she still seemed to be in such a bad way. But I had trusted these people so far, and they hadn't let us down; this was no time not to listen to them. The truth is that I was simply afraid. And while I was nervous about a move, it actually was a positive sign that she was improving. It's all a matter of perspective.

Sharon could not go to a rehabilitation facility, as she had no motor activity, and certainly could not come home, as she was still dependent on the ventilator. And so began the search for a long-term care facility that would be able to care for a ventilator patient. There were only two that were within a reasonable distance. Granted, the major issue was quality of care, but since Ann and I had to be there every day, we had to be realistic and factor geography into the equation.

I began to do some research so I would know what to look for when I visited the two facilities and typed up several pages of questions that I had. I would not be content to take the "nickel tour." I wanted to meet and talk to the people that would be taking care of my wife.

I remember well the first facility Ann and I visited. It seemed nice enough, but when I pulled out my list of questions (several pages), I saw the representative from admissions wince a little. I guess he hadn't been expecting so many questions or such detailed questions. I explained politely that I wasn't buying a barbecue grill; I was looking for a facility to keep my wife alive. So, yes, I had *a lot* of questions! I went through my list one by one. Some questions he was able to answer, and some he would need to get back to me about. We thanked him for his time and went on our way to our next appointment.

The next stop on the itinerary took us to Saint Agnes Long-Term Intensive Care Hospital in South Philadelphia. Ann and I met with Kathy Hoffman, the director in the admissions department. Kathy had been at Saint Agnes for over three decades and was also a registered nurse, so that gave me confidence right away. Kathy took us on a tour of the hospital, as I would have expected, but then threw me a curve ball. She *insisted* that we meet with the nursing manager, Paula Solipaca. Already I was impressed!

Given the gravity of the situation, I jumped at the chance to meet the person who would be directly involved with Sharon's case. Paula too had been at Saint Agnes for a number of years, and that's as good of a guess as I can give. I only say that because she stated that she had worked there since she was a teenager. I wasn't about to try to put an actual number on it, as it is generally considered bad form to guess a woman's age. The results can be disastrous! Suffice to say that I felt confident with her experience there.

Paula made us feel comfortable right away, as Ann and I explained to her what we were looking for in the way of care for Sharon. I explained to Paula that my medical credentials were very basic; I had most of the common childhood maladies, I was a former Emergency Medical Technician, and I had been a spinal-cord patient (the school of hard knocks). That's the extent of my medical training! However, given my experiences, I felt that I was qualified to play a vital role in this process. I explained to Paula my feelings regarding infection control, skin care, and physical therapy as I went through my multi-page list of questions. Paula dealt with each question in a professional manner and was eager to work with us.

I had only two other prerequisites, the first of which was that I wanted the best doctor on Sharon's case. The doctors are normally assigned on a rotation basis as patients come in. I flat-out asked Paula if she would break rotation and make sure Sharon had the best. She assured me that the medical director, Doctor Dovnarsky, would oversee Sharon's care.

My second prerequisite was that I was not to be treated by anyone as simply the visiting spouse. I was to be viewed as part of the team. This, in my opinion, was not negotiable. Too often hospital personnel ask you to leave the room when they will be doing things with the patient. I would leave the room for nothing and expected to be informed of everything and involved in all communications. The same would apply to Ann. She was to be in the loop on everything. Paula shook our hands and welcomed us aboard, and really the decision was made at that point as to what Sharon's next step would be.

I must admit, however, that I was somewhat nervous about transferring Sharon.

All right, that's not true. I was *really* nervous about transferring Sharon. The truth is that Ann and I were making decisions regarding her care, and basically, her life was in our hands. Her condition was still critical, and I had concerns about her leaving the step-down unit at Jefferson. Sharon's blood pressure was spiking, she had developed tremors in her head and neck, and she was pretty much riding the ventilator, meaning that it was doing all of the work.

I continued to pray for Sharon's recovery as well as for my own strength. I knew that within a week it was expected that Sharon would have to be transferred. I just prayed that she would be ready when the time came and that I would continue to make all of the right choices, along with Ann's help. I was doing my best to keep things in perspective, as I knew that this was going to be a long uphill battle.

As we made our way into the first week of June, Sharon was starting to do a little bit of breathing on her own. She was still connected to the ventilator, but the respiratory therapists would switch it over to a mode where it would only activate if it needed to.

Otherwise, Sharon would do the breathing. She did a few short spells, which left her very fatigued. But it was progress! She was taking some breaths on her own, and that's what mattered. I was very excited, as it had been over a month since she had taken a breath unassisted. I was very proud of her and of how hard she was working to get better and to keep a positive attitude. Moving day was quickly approaching, and that would mark another milestone for Sharon.

Plane crashes

A Media man flying out of Avondale was seriously injured in a plane crash Sunday.

Robert Hanlon, no age given, was admitted to the trauma center at Lancaster General Hospital and was in surgery for a back injury Sunday night, according to police and hospital spokeswomen.

The small two-seater craft Hanlon was piloting appeared to lose power and crash landed in a cornfield in Little Britain Township, Lancaster County, at about 2 p.m., according to Gregory Bledsoe, deputy chief of the Quarryville Fire Co.

Bledsoe said the wings and front section of the airplane were bent.

(Left) This is what is known as having a really bad day. *(Reprint courtesy of Daily Local News - West Chester, PA)*

(Below) September 9, 1990—They say that any landing you can walk away from is a good one, and if the airplane is still useable, the landing was a great one. Unfortunately, I did not accomplish either. *(Reprint courtesy of Intelligencer Journal - Lancaster, PA)*

BOY, 1, SUFFERS A CUT.
A one-year-old boy suffered
a cut on the forehead last night
when he fell on the edge of a
one-gallon can at the home.
Robert Hanlon, son of Mr. and
Mrs. John P. Hanlon, jr., 7856
Tomahawk road, Prairie Village, was treated at the University of Kansas Medical Center.

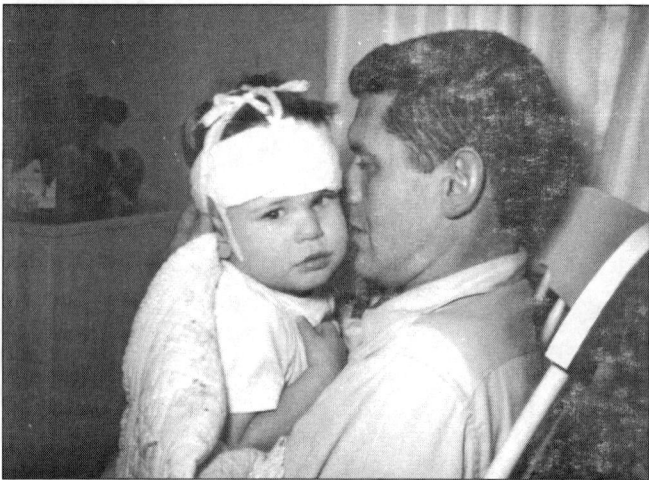

With my father during the early days in Kansas, already
busting myself up and making the newspaper. Could this
be just a little prophetic? *(Reprint courtesy of Kansas City Star
– Kansas City, MO)*

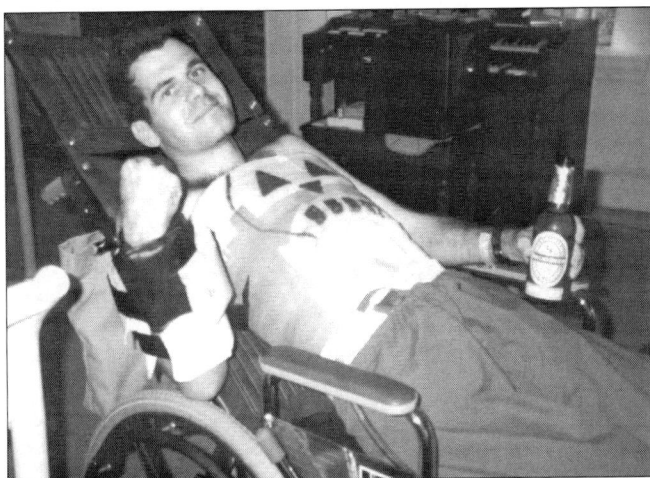

November 1990 - In my body cast, exercising. My workout routine was anything but balanced; I had sixteen pounds strapped to my right arm but only sixteen ounces on the other side!

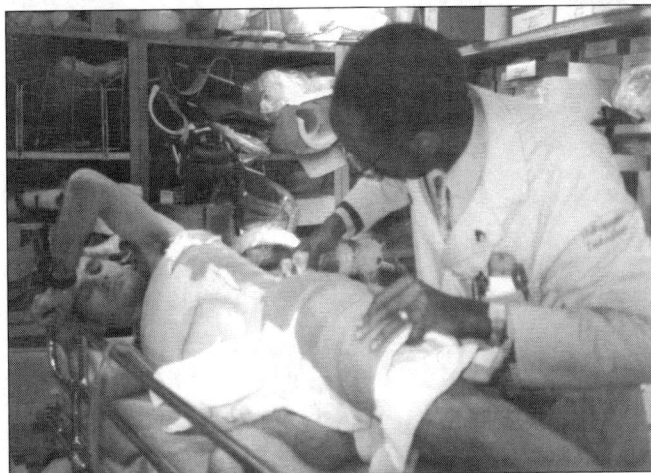

December 3, 1990—In the cast room at Jefferson Hospital with Tony and his cast saw. I was finally getting out of my "shell."

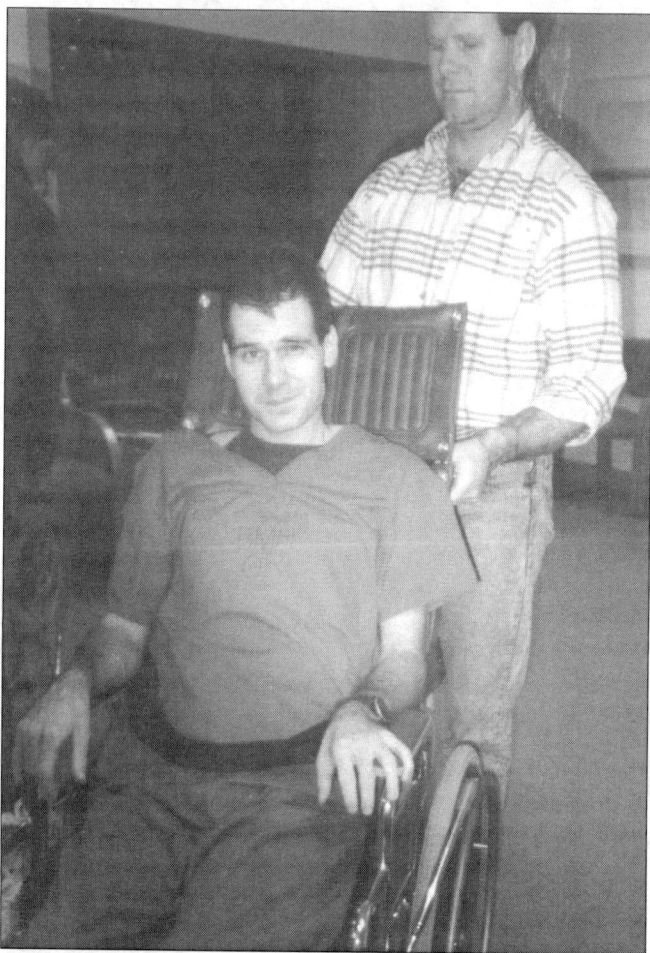

With my brother Jack, just minutes out of my cast. I looked and felt like a refugee, having lost forty pounds. Can anybody spare a few dozen cheeseburgers?

September 29, 1996—Our wedding day. Ain't she gorgeous?

Sharon, circa 2000, stopping for a quick photo with me before she takes off into the wild blue yonder.

Singing country music at Hennessy's Restaurant—Aston, PA

April 29, 2006—Photo of us taken just four hours before Sharon went to the hospital. It is hard to imagine that just twenty-four hours later, she was totally paralyzed and on life support.

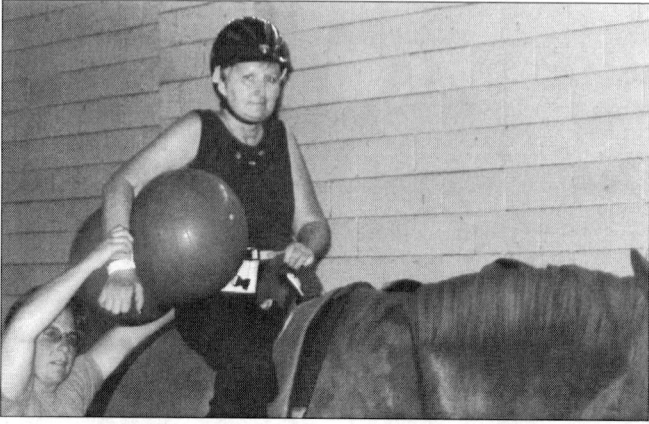

August 22, 2006—Sharon riding Libby at Thorncroft Stables during equestrian therapy.

September 19, 2006—Sharon walking out of Bryn Mawr Rehab on the day she was discharged. The journey was long, but it was finally time to go home. We had prayed for this day, and God was listening.

The Biggest Hurdle

June 7, 2006 arrived before we knew it, and we were packing Sharon up in order to make the transfer to Saint Agnes Hospital. We really had one goal in mind with this move, and that goal was for Sharon to successfully wean off of the ventilator. I was apprehensive but also excited at the same time.

It is amazing how many things one can accumulate while in the hospital, even while on life support. I had packed up most of the things the night before so the move would be simple. The transport team arrived at the appointed time, transferred Sharon to a stretcher, and then connected her to a portable battery-operated ventilator. Yes, a battery-operated ventilator! The only thought running through my mind was that I was hoping they had really good batteries in it. Yeah, I worry too much.

It was a generally cloudy day, and by the time the transport team got Sharon outside to the ambulance, it had begun to rain. I was worried about Sharon getting rained on, but she later told me that it actually felt good to have the rain hitting her face. It had been over five weeks since she had been outside in the fresh air, that is, if you can call the air in the city fresh.

But it was better than in the hospital room. Hospitals are always so hot, and we actually had put a big fan in Sharon's room to keep her comfortable. So even a little "fresh city air" was a welcome relief for her. The ride across town only took a few minutes, and we promptly arrived at Saint Agnes Hospital and moved Sharon up to her room on the fourth floor. I immediately met with Doctor Brody, who was one of the members of Doctor Dovnarsky's team. Paula had kept her word and had assigned Sharon's case to the best team, not that I ever doubted her.

It didn't take very long for me to let everybody know how I wanted things to be done. I have no doubt that somewhere along the way I may have ruffled a few feathers. But to be truthful, I was very clear about the fact that I wasn't running for public office. If somebody didn't like the way I did things, so be it. My job was to keep Sharon alive and help her get better, and as we've all heard many times, the squeaky wheel gets the oil.

Sharon quickly adjusted to her new surroundings and was delighted when we moved her bed around so she could at least see out the window. The summer of 2006 was a scorcher, and even the best of air conditioners struggled with the temperatures. So I added a second fan to her room, in addition to getting her CD player hooked up. Sharon loves the ocean and the beach, so I would put on a CD at night that had sounds of the ocean and seagulls so she could go to her special favorite place. All she had to do was close her eyes and listen. The highlight of the day was that she moved her hips and her legs the slightest bit. It wasn't much, but she was moving; it was a step in the right direction.

My next order of business was to familiarize myself with all of the equipment in Sharon's room. The ventilator and the machine that supplied her feeding tube were different from what she had been connected to at Jefferson, so I had to learn what all of the functions were. Yes, I drove some of the staff crazy. I had no desire to do anything with the equipment; I just simply wanted to know how it worked so I could recognize a problem if there ever was one.

By the end of her first week, Sharon had some issues with highly elevated pulse and blood pressure, as well as the tremors that still persisted. They called to tell me that her blood pressure had gone through the roof, and a cardiologist was going to see her. I was extremely worried about the risk of a stroke, for her and me! I hurried downtown, expecting the worst. Little did I know, the cardiologist had already been there and changed some of her medication. I walked into her room expecting to see her at death's door, and she briskly turned her head, winked at me with the eye that didn't have a patch on it, tried to make the biggest smile that she could, and puckered up to tell me that she wanted a kiss!

Obviously the new medications had taken effect quickly. If I hadn't known better, I'd have sworn that she was trying to give *me* a heart attack or stroke. I was making phone calls on my way there to get a priest to administer the Last Rites because I was afraid she would die, and she played cute when I got there. Ain't it great!

Not yet content, Sharon decided to show off a

little bit. She turned her head back and forth, nod-ded, winked at me, stuck her tongue out at me, shrugged her shoulders, wiggled her hips, and even lifted her head off of the pillow the slightest bit. I was so excited! She was starting to get a lot of motor activity back as nerves regenerated and consistently would move any part of her body that she could in order to exercise the muscles.

The next scene was priceless. I could tell she wanted something, so I grabbed the board and a marker. Remember the board I talked about with the alphabet on it? I pointed to letters, and she blinked when I picked the right one. So I start pointing and writing down letters as she blinked her eyes. What did she spell? P-L-A-T-T-E-R! She didn't spell out "food" or even spell out "I'm hungry." No, not Sha-ron; she went right for "platter!"

All I could think was that this poor girl must really be hungry to come up with that. Not that I could blame her, since it was June 14 and her last meal had been April 29.

She also spelled out that she wanted a frozen mar-garita. She loves those frozen beverages. She always says that they are "fun." I considered her cocktail order to be a positive sign that she was on the mend! But it was going to have to wait.

We were so grateful for the progress that she was making, and every night gave thanks.

We always made it a point to say our prayers together before I would leave the hospital every night, although Sharon just moved her lips and I had to do the sound part since she couldn't speak yet. But as long as your lips are moving, it still counts! God knows when you are talking to Him.

Within a few days, unfortunately, Sharon hit another obstacle in the form of a partially collapsed lung. I was getting ready to head out to the hospital when Doctor Brody called me to let me know what was going on. She assured me that she could easily take care of it. Apparently, she noticed the problem due to the readings on the ventilator machine and caught it before Sharon ever got into distress. This crew was definitely on top of their game, which I was really glad about. It was a fairly simple procedure to take care of the lung, and Sharon was not even aware that it had happened. I, on the other hand, was feeling just about stretched to the limit. Every time Sharon would make progress, something would happen to set her back.

I recall praying and asking God just how much Sharon was supposed to endure. While the collapsed lung was not a painful experience for Sharon, it set the process of weaning off of the ventilator back almost a week. I happened to be with my brother Jack when I received the phone call from Dr. Brody. I was truly at my wit's end, and Jack asked me if there was anything that he could do. I responded by telling him that he needed to go home, hug his wife and that precious daughter of his (his daughter, Isabelle, is a sweetie), never let go of them, and treasure every moment that he has with them.

Life is too short, and we never know what tomorrow will bring. As funny as it may sound, I remember telling Jack to treasure even those little things that his wife and daughter might do that drive him crazy. Those little things would probably be the first things that we would miss if something happened to a loved one. If you're married or have children, you know what I mean. If you are single and childless, just wait! I believe that time will prove me right and that you will understand what I mean.

Every day was a new lesson in faith and courage. I kept my Bible at Sharon's bedside so I could read from it while at the hospital and found that to be a great source of strength. The night before the collapsed lung incident, I had been reading about Moses going to face the Pharaoh to demand the release of the Israelites. Moses wasn't exactly thrilled to be chosen and believed that his brother Aaron was better suited for the job. Moses did not consider himself to be a good speaker and didn't believe that anyone would listen to him. God assured Moses that he would be with him, just as I had to have faith and keep believing that God would stay by us.

And of course, as we all know from the story, after Moses agreed to go, God said "But I will harden his heart, so that he will not let the people go" (Exodus 4:21). Somehow I believe that Moses probably could have done without the additional challenge. However, I believe that there are several lessons that come out of this story:

1. Had God not challenged Moses, then Moses could not have become the leader that he was. I believe he had it in him all of the time, just as we all have untapped strength and abilities within us. We need to stretch and grow as Moses did and develop those qualities. We can never achieve great things if we remain in our comfort zone.

2. Had Moses not grown and become a strong leader, perhaps the Israelites would not have followed him and would have remained in captivity. I believe that this applies to everyday life. I do not believe that leaders are born. True leaders are the result of people who have chosen to grow.

3. Had it been that simple for the Israelites to leave captivity, there would be nothing to learn from the story of Moses, and it would have made a lousy movie. Okay, just a thought.

Humor aside, the point of all of this is that when we face adversities, we must always surrender ourselves into God's hands and trust that he will carry us through. God has a plan for all of us. Yes, it means that we must leave our comfort zone, and we must develop the fighting spirit that we all have inside of us.

Sharon's courage, strength, and faith were amazing. While I could sense at times that she was afraid, she never gave up. But there is nothing wrong with being afraid. It is a very normal reaction. It keeps us alive. Pop always said that you never want to follow a guy into battle that isn't just a little bit afraid, because he's going to get *your* head shot off. I look at being afraid as a sign that you still have all of your marbles.

Although she couldn't speak at the time, she later told me that there was never a point when she thought that she was not going to get through this. She said that she knew it would be a long process but knew without a doubt that she would triumph. I have since pointed out to her jokingly that she couldn't see how sick she looked, which is probably a good thing!

Sharon said that she simply put herself in God's hands and asked Him to watch over her. It was painful to watch her struggle, but believe it or not, I give thanks to God for choosing me to go through this ordeal with her. Given my experiences following my airplane accident, I had a fairly good idea of some of the things that she was feeling and of some of the things that would need to be dealt with. That is, of course, excluding the ventilator. That is something I have not and hope to not ever experience firsthand. But her pain was my pain, and we were going to get through this together.

By June 23, the respiratory team began to try weaning Sharon from the ventilator. She had been resting for five days after her "event," as they call it. I always found that term to be quite amusing. Whenever something went wrong, they would tell me that Sharon had an event. Call me crazy, but when I think of an event, I think of a carnival, a sports game, or perhaps a cookout. A collapsed lung does not come to mind! I guess that is their way of downplaying it so it doesn't sound too serious. I would rather they just hit me in the head with a hammer and give me the news. I can handle it. Either way, I was glad that Sharon was past it and was back to trying to breathe on her own.

Sharon was only able to do three hours of breathing the first day but was able to increase that the next day, doing three hours in the morning and three hours in the evening. With each day came an increase in the amount of time that Sharon was able to breathe on her own without relying on the ventilator. Fatigue was still a constant factor, but she pushed herself to the limit. We simply took one day at a time and dealt with each issue that came up one by one.

We were surrounded by people that were a constant source of strength and help. It was as if we had a constant supply of guardian angels. During the times that Sharon would suffer setbacks though, I sometimes wondered if God was hearing our prayers. And then it occurred to me one night that possibly there was someone else who needed a miracle too and didn't have anyone praying for them or that it just wasn't our turn yet. I would constantly read the verse about the footprints in the sand. Although some days it felt as if we were face down in the sand, I always saw a set of footprints, so I knew that God was carrying us.

———

Sharon seemed to be having a rough time getting back in stride with trying to wean from the ventilator. I think that she was a little nervous knowing that the ventilator would be switched over and she would be doing all of the work. The machine wasn't turned off; it was simply switched into a mode where Sharon would breathe on her own, but it would kick in and help her if she got into trouble. For a few days, every time the machine was switched over, Sharon got nervous, had trouble getting started, and wouldn't be able to breathe on her own, and then the alarms on the machine would spook her a little bit.

So the next morning, when the respiratory therapist came in, she told Sharon that she was just checking all of the settings on the machine but switched it off without telling her. Sharon was completely unaware of the change and went the whole day breathing on her own. She was still connected but was not aware that she was doing all of the work.

Throughout the day, I would mention about getting started weaning again soon, as I didn't want to give up the little secret. I never told her that she was already doing it on her own. Yes, I was telling my wife a little white lie, but I had no choice in this case.

Finally, Sharon had the ability and the confidence to try to be totally independent. So the team turned off the ventilator and disconnected the hoses from her. For one hour Sharon was breathing completely on her own and with no crutch to lean on. While she had been doing fine before, she had the ventilator to fall back on. This was a huge step for her psychologically.

I often use flying to illustrate many points, partly

because I like airplanes but also because so many things we do compare with aspects of flying. This day was similar to Sharon making her first solo flight. When you solo in an airplane, you don't do anything different than you've already done, with the exception that now the seat next to you is *empty!* There is no longer an instructor there to help you. You have no choice but to do it right, and there is definitely some psychological difference in knowing that you are doing it alone. Sharon was breathing just as she had on previous days, but she knew that she was disconnected and handled the challenge just fine.

I remember talking with Sharon about one aspect of her flight training when she was having some apprehension about weaning from the ventilator. Very early on in her training, she was expressing some concerns because she had heard someone talking about doing their long cross-country trip. One of the training requirements in those days called for the student to do a three-hundred-mile trip *alone!* At the time, Sharon's only response was, "I can't do that! I don't even know how to land the airplane by myself!"

I told her that it was all right, because she wasn't going to have to do it the next day. She wasn't even going to do it the following month. All that she needed to do was take each lesson and use it as a building block, and when she was ready, we would then deal with the long cross-country. And it wouldn't happen until she knew she was ready and until Jimmy knew she was ready. After all, the instructor has to sign off that someone is truly prepared.

And so it was with the ventilator. I assured her that nobody was going to take the ventilator away and "make her fly solo" if she wasn't ready. She would take one day at a time, do what she could, and use that as a building block.

Despite the fact that Sharon ended up handling it all just fine, the respiratory therapist only left Sharon disconnected for the one hour. We didn't want her to get fatigued and then get into distress. The goal was for Sharon to be independent of the ventilator, but the key thing here was that she needed to be ready and willing to try it again. Being scared doesn't usually make people want to try something again. Sadly, I've had many people tell me that they went for their first airplane ride, and for some reason they ended up being scared out of their minds and never wanting to fly again. We wanted Sharon to actually look forward to being disconnected from the ventilator, not to be afraid of it.

So we took baby steps and worked at a comfortable pace. I remember at one point Sharon had spent an entire day and well into the evening disconnected, and although she was doing well, I had the respiratory therapist connect her back up to the ventilator.

She was doing so well, and I just didn't want to risk having her get into trouble. Fortunately, they always listened to my thoughts and opinions, and then collectively we would decide the best course of action for Sharon. I am forever grateful to the staff for treating me as an equal. They were true professionals.

As we moved into July, a lot was happening. Sharon was getting stronger and breathing more on her own, she was starting to move her arms and legs a bit, and fortunately I was getting better at reading lips. The marker board that we had been using for months was effective, but it was also very time consuming to point to all of the letters, have Sharon blink her eyes, and then try to make sentences.

The one challenge with reading lips was that Sharon's facial muscles had been affected, so her lips were difficult to read sometimes, as they didn't move as they once did. Added to this challenge was the fact that Sharon did not realize that her lips didn't move in unison, making her wonder just why the heck we were having such difficulty understanding her.

Sharon was starting to show her sarcastic side. I arrived at the hospital one day to find Ann there trying to communicate with her using the letter board. Ann was really struggling trying to figure out what Sharon was trying to say, between using the board and trying to read her lips. This went on for about ten minutes, and Ann was having absolutely zero success reading Sharon's lips. Finally, I asked Sharon what was on her mind, and she mouthed the words to me. I think it was only a matter of luck, but I got it on the first try. The look she gave Ann was priceless. It was almost as if she was saying, "Idiot, what's your problem? Bob got it right away!" The moment was priceless, and it was the first time in quite a while that any of us had laughed until it hurt.

Sharon then indicated that she wanted something to eat, but that wasn't possible yet. I had never seen her bottom lip stick out so far in all of the time I've known her. She had quite a serious pout! Once again, we all shared a great laugh; things were looking up. It felt good to have her back.

Sharon's next question was a tough one. Someone might as well have driven a stake through my heart. Her question was, "When are *we* planning to go home?" It was a difficult moment for me. I knew deep down that she was so very tired of all of this, and believe me when I tell you that nobody wanted her to come home more than I did. But she still had a long way to go. I hugged her closely and told her that we had a few more hurdles to clear but that it wouldn't be much longer. She was getting past the biggest hurdle, the ventilator. I just didn't have the heart to tell her at that moment that she was going to have one more hospital to go to before coming home. She remained stoic and took everything in stride. She knew that all of this was only temporary. I sometimes envied her for the strength that she showed.

Sharon was always up for a challenge and never gave up trying. One night I was having a challenge reading her lips, so I used the marker board. She spelled out "Give me the marker." She wanted to try to write the words herself. She wasn't able to write or even hold the marker yet, but she tried with all of her might.

She finally indicated that she was thirsty but didn't want to use a sponge. Up to this point, the only way to quench her thirst was to use a small sponge on a stick. We would dip it in water and put it on her lips and in her mouth. That wasn't going to suffice at this point. She was fed up with sucking on a sponge. So I got a straw and put it in a cup of water, and surprise of surprises, she managed to get water up the straw and into her mouth to swallow it! A few times I had to suction her, as she had gotten a little overzealous and took in too much water. But she was getting the job done!

It goes without saying that the hospital staff had no knowledge that I was doing this. For some reason they tend to get real uptight about liability and things being done that aren't protocol. I can't say that I blame them. But we always figured that as long as you know the rules, then you know how to break them. And it's always better to beg for forgiveness than to ask for permission. But please don't try this at home; we only *think* that we are trained professionals!

On July 12, 2006, I heard the sweetest sound that I have ever experienced. The respiratory therapy team had Sharon disconnected from the ventilator and had put a Passy-Muir valve onto her tracheotomy tube. This is a valve that allowed her to inhale through the tracheotomy tube but exhale normally, allowing her vocal cords to work. Basically, it is a one-way valve. I walked into her room and was totally surprised when she said, "Hi, honey!" I must admit that I cried when I heard the sound of her voice. It had been several months since Sharon had been able to speak, so this was a very special moment, one that was a long time coming.

It was an exciting day for everyone. Doctor Dovnarsky had come into Sharon's room and was not aware that she was talking, as he had not viewed her chart yet. Sharon looked up and said, "Hello, Doctor," kind of catching him off guard. He was so excited to hear her speak that he kind of did this little dance. He was a happy camper! We were all happy campers!

Suddenly it seemed as if Sharon had hit a critical point, and things started to happen quickly. She was talking, as well as regaining substantial motor activity in her extremities. We even tried some arm wrestling, and she beat me! I guess there's not much chance that I will ever grace the front of a cereal box for my athletic prowess. Sharon is sure that I let her beat me, and I'm not admitting to anything.

Of course all of this progress meant one thing— Sharon was going to be leaving Saint Agnes Hospital in the foreseeable future and going to another facility for physical therapy. Within a week of Sharon starting to talk, the staff rolled the ventilator out of her room, and we said good-bye to that machine forever. Sharon still had the tracheotomy cannula in her neck, as they didn't want to pull that out until everyone was certain that she was strong enough. It's not the kind of thing that you want to remove and then have to say, "Oops,

I think we jumped the gun a little. We better put it back in." Once it is out, it stays out. Not that it can't go back in, it just wouldn't be a whole lot of fun for the patient. The Passy-Muir valve was removed and the tube was capped off, so Sharon was inhaling and exhaling normally at that point.

We were just taking precautions to make sure that she was strong enough to breathe completely on her own and that she could cough on her own, as we would not be able to suction her once the tracheotomy cannula was removed. Within a few days, Sharon coughed so hard that she blew the cap right off of the cannula, and the best part was that we couldn't even find it! I think it must have flown out the window and landed somewhere on Mifflin Street. We all agreed at that point that she was strong enough to have the tracheotomy removed, which was accomplished on July 26. The process is actually simpler than most would think. No big procedure, no stitches. All they do is slide the cannula out of her neck, and the trachea and the incision in the skin just close up all on their own.

I continued to be impressed at how the staff involved me and listened to my opinion on decisions regarding Sharon's care. One of the respiratory therapists told me that everybody in the hospital knew who I was. I laughed and asked her, "Is that a good thing?" She assured me that it was. I'll take her word for it, as I remember getting off of the elevator one evening and having one of the nurses salute me and address me as "commander in chief." Of course

I know that she was teasing me, and before long the title caught on with several of the other staff.

They were a fabulous team and were great to work with. The nursing staff, especially Theo and Christine, looked after Sharon as if she were family. But we were days away from having to say good-bye. They had done their job successfully, as Sharon was free from the ventilator and was breathing on her own. Their work was done.

Physical Rehab—
Country Style

July 31, 2006 marked another milestone for Sharon, as we transferred her to Bryn Mawr Rehab located in Malvern, Pennsylvania. It is a beautiful facility nestled in the countryside out in Chester County. Being a country boy, I was as happy as a pig in a mudslide. Sharon was happy with the choice as well. She is not much of a city person either, and now she would be able to go outside and enjoy the scenery, as she was no longer tied to all of the life-support equipment. Sharon's never been real big on the mudslide thing, though.

The truth is that I would have transferred Sharon to whichever facility I believed would be best for her. It just turned out to be a winning hand for everyone. We had found a first-class facility that was in a desirable location. I was extremely tired of the city, and I knew that Sharon would be more comfortable with our choice.

Ann and I had visited Bryn Mawr Rehab the previous Friday to tour the facility and met with Clare Small-McEvoy, one of the physical therapy (PT) coordinators. I was immediately impressed with Clare's professionalism and her positive attitude regarding the goals we had for Sharon. It goes without saying that the goal was for Sharon to walk out of the hospital on the day of her discharge. I realize that nobody has a crystal ball or can forecast somebody's level of recovery, but I was looking for a team that would support our goals and work with Sharon in a positive manner. We weren't there for more than fifteen minutes when Ann and I made our decision that this was where Sharon needed to be.

On our way downtown to see Sharon, I called the case manager at Saint Agnes to let her know of our choice so she could set the wheels in motion for the transfer. To my amazement, someone from Bryn Mawr had already been in touch and was on their way to do a physical evaluation of Sharon in preparation for transfer on Monday. I was impressed. Sharon later told me that the whole time Ann and I were out touring Bryn Mawr Rehab, she was sending us positive vibes to make that the choice. She really wanted to go there.

Sunday morning I went shopping before going to the hospital to be with Sharon. I wanted to get her some new clothes that would be comfortable to wear while exercising in therapy. This was a new experience for me, as I had never shopped for any of Sharon's clothing. It was quite a funny experience, and believe me, it is a story that can only be told in person! Trust me.

Other than the fact that July 31 was probably the hottest day of the summer of 2006, the transfer went smoothly, except that the air-conditioning in the ambulance wasn't keeping pace with the temperatures. Sharon later told me how uncomfortable the ride was. I was not in the ambulance as I had them follow me since I knew a shortcut and wanted the ride to be as brief as possible. Come to think of it, my air conditioner wasn't keeping pace either. It was a beasty day!

As I drove along with the ambulance behind me, my mind wandered. Once again I was just slightly anxious about the transfer, as I always had to remember that Sharon's life was in my hands and that much of her outcome would be a direct result of my decisions. I just kept hoping and praying that I would make all of the right ones. But so far everything had worked out, and Sharon had been happy with all of the choices that Ann and I had made.

Upon arrival at Bryn Mawr, Sharon was moved to her room on the Spruce Unit (all of the hospital wings are named after trees—I guess it's a country thing), where we promptly got her settled in. I immediately felt comfortable as we were welcomed by various staff members. I knew Sharon was going to be in great hands and that we would have a good working relationship. On my initial meeting and tour with Clare, I had been very clear about how I needed to be involved in all aspects of patient care—part of the team. The staff on the Spruce Unit was wonderful when it came to working together.

I met the two doctors who would be caring for Sharon: Doctor Kraus would be overseeing the physical therapy portion of her care, and Doctor Saperstein would be tending to her medical needs. I was immediately comfortable with both of them. Good thing too, because I'm not sure what I would have done otherwise. I sure as heck couldn't bring her home yet. But my mind was at ease knowing that Ann and I had made the best choice. Once again Sharon was in the right place with the right people.

Tuesday was Sharon's first full day at Bryn Mawr Rehab, and we met her physical therapist, Megan Gibbons, an absolutely sweet girl. I discussed our goals with Megan, as I felt it was important for her to understand, right out of the gate, where we were headed and for all of us to know what to expect from one another. Fortunately, Megan was right on track with us and bonded with Sharon immediately. Come to think of it, everybody always bonded with Sharon right away and ultimately became very protective of her. She just has that effect on people. Everybody loves Sharon.

One of the first things the staff did was to stand Sharon up and take her blood pressure. It would be her first time standing in three months, and they wanted to see how her pressure would be affected. Of course they had to hold her up as she had very little strength in her legs. While they had Sharon out of bed, they sat her in a wheelchair as they took that opportunity to change to a different-style bed.

I had a nice conversation with the doctors and nurses and explained what I had done up to this point to maintain Sharon's condition. And I certainly was hoping to continue doing things the same way, as everything had worked well so far. The rate of infection had been minimal (it is rare that infection is completely avoidable during a lengthy hospital stay), and her muscles and range of motion were fairly good for a patient that had been sedentary for three months. The admitting nurse had marveled at how good her skin looked. Sharon was not going to have skin problems on my watch, and it didn't take any convincing at all, hence the immediate change to an air bed just as we had done at Saint Agnes. It was the beginning of a great working relationship.

While the staff was putting the new bed into Sharon's room, I took her for a little tour of the grounds. What a sight we were! There I was, with my cane and my mediocre ability to walk, pushing Sharon around in a wheelchair. No doubt people were curious, judging by the looks on their faces. Sharon enjoyed the little ride and was happy to be out and about, as she had spent three months in a bed. I know that she was glad to see something other than the ceiling. I could relate, given the amount of time I spent lying flat out in my body cast.

The next morning the staff had Sharon up and out at seven thirty, and she did a full schedule of therapy, only breaking for lunch, ending up back in her room a little after four in the afternoon. They had her standing again at one point; however, her blood pressure dropped significantly, so they sat her back down. By the end of the day, Sharon was fairly exhausted, and I had been up all night getting things done so I was well past exhausted.

Before long I was in the bed next to Sharon, and

we were both asleep. This would become a common thing for us as Sharon would be fatigued from therapy, and I was usually getting only two to three hours of sleep a night at best. The nurses thought it was so cute, but for us it was survival.

Within a few days Sharon became ill and had to take it easy. She still had the feeding tube in her, and to be truthful, I think her system had about all that it could take from it. She still wasn't eating anything yet as she had not been evaluated for her ability to swallow.

Because of the extent of the Guillain-Barré, she would have to learn how to chew and swallow all over again. I was convinced that a cheesesteak (that's a Philly thing) and a water ice (another Philly thing) would settle her stomach, but the doctors weren't quite ready to take my word on that one. They wanted to rule out any other illness (also an excellent plan). I just knew how badly Sharon wanted to try to eat something, as she was so hungry. I started becoming the squeaky wheel and finally got someone's attention about having

Sharon evaluated. Within a few hours, one of the speech therapists came to see Sharon to evaluate her ability to swallow. Sharon ate some pudding, crackers, and cereal successfully. The area of concern was that patients can sometimes aspirate food; however, the speech therapist listened to Sharon swallowing using a stethoscope and was very pleased with the results. Sharon was finally cleared to eat soft food!

Unfortunately, because of the lack of manual dexterity, Sharon couldn't feed herself but was grateful to be able to have real food, even if it meant having someone help her. I felt certain that it wouldn't be long before Sharon could hold utensils, as she was starting to make great strides. She was able to operate the controls on the television, which was something that she hadn't been able to do before.

Within a week of Sharon being cleared to eat, I threw all caution to the wind and brought her a chicken cheesesteak. Naturally this was, once again, without the knowledge or approval of the doctors (you have to break the rules once in a while). She enjoyed half of it but got full very quickly as her stomach wasn't used to having food in it, as it had been well over three months since she had eaten. Sharon was very happy and was looking forward to trying pizza.

Sharon continued to do well in therapy and to get stronger but was struggling with her blood pressure when the therapists would try to stand her up. They were using what is called a "tilt table" to bring Sharon up to a standing position gradually. Every time they would raise her partway up and her blood pressure would drop, they would put her back down. Sharon never experienced any other difficulties or symptoms regarding her blood pressure and just wanted to proceed without the tilt table and all of the blood pressure checks. She saw the tilt table as an impediment and would have gladly burned that device to the ground. All she wanted to do was stand up and try to walk, right away.

Then one day about two weeks into therapy, Sharon was working with a different therapist because of scheduling issues. Megan was doing a terrific job with Sharon, but it never hurts to get another person's perspective. Joann seemed to have a real grab-the-bull-by-the-horns attitude and said to Sharon, "Let's try something crazy." She rolled Sharon over to the parallel bars, locked the wheels on the wheelchair, and told Sharon to pull herself up. The worst that could happen is Sharon would sit right back down in the wheelchair. Summoning every bit of strength she had, Sharon grabbed the bar, pulled herself to a standing position three times, and stood for a total of five minutes without assistance!

I am sorry that I was not there to witness that, but by the time I got there, the hospital was buzzing with excitement. Everybody I talked to was grinning ear to ear and saying to me, "Sharon stood today!" It was truly touching how everybody took such a personal interest in Sharon, even those that were not directly caring for her. I would expect those charged with her care and treatment to be excited, but everyone else as well was genuinely enthusiastic about her progress.

This was Sharon's turning point. She announced to everybody that she no longer wanted anybody to do anything for her unless they felt she was in danger of falling or hurting herself. Sharon had cleared another major hurdle and, in doing so, raised her confidence level. She didn't need anybody to "raise the bar" for her; she raised it for herself. At that point, she believed that she could in fact walk out of the hospital. There was no stopping her now—she was a woman on a mission!

I was so proud of Sharon. She was accomplishing so much and maintaining a great attitude throughout all that was happening. I have to honestly say that I am, without a doubt, the luckiest man in the world. God truly blessed me when he sent Sharon to me.

But it was bittersweet to watch her struggle, as each struggle meant progress as well as being painful and frustrating to Sharon. I would have gladly taken her place if I could have, but since that was not an option, all I could do was help take care of her and try to be a source of strength and support.

Sharon continued to work as hard as she could since we had set a deadline for her to walk. It wasn't good enough to say that Sharon would walk again soon or someday. In five weeks Sharon would need to walk through the front doors of the hospital to go home.

That was the goal, just as it had been my goal when I was in the hospital years earlier.

The hard work fatigued her, and we had to be careful not to push her too hard. The last thing we wanted was for Sharon to get hurt and suffer any setbacks.

Sharon would usually take a nap at lunchtime and in between therapy sessions. After we would have dinner, I usually ended up in my typical spot, next to her in the bed, and we would cuddle up and take a nap. Before going home at the end of the evening, I would always give Sharon her shower and take care of her hair. She was looking forward to when she would be able to do those things herself, as I'm no hairstylist! I was able to hold my own doing her nails though. I gave Sharon a new color on her nails every week just to keep it interesting. One of the nurses suggested that I set up a kiosk in the lobby selling manicures. I took a pass on that one.

It may seem odd to some for me to say that we enjoyed our time at Bryn Mawr Rehab.

But since we had to be there, we made the best of it, and to be truthful, that didn't require any effort. Everybody treated Sharon wonderfully and treated me as one of their own. I always wore at least one, if not both, of the two badges I had that read "I Love Nurses" and "Nurses Rock!" One day I had forgotten to wear my badge, and I was chided for being out of uniform. I never slipped up again! The nurses looked forward to seeing those badges on me.

Sharon looked forward to dinner every day as the food there was actually pretty good. It wasn't your typical hospital food that requires being sent to a laboratory to identify.

Even so, sometimes I would get takeout from some of the local establishments just to round out our diet a little. Whenever I would get pizza, I would let staff know ahead of time what day it would be so they didn't pack lunch or dinner. Then I would have a half dozen or so large pizzas delivered to the Spruce Unit so the staff could enjoy some as well.

The nurses and the techs (aides) were very special, and buying them dinner now and then was my way of showing our appreciation, although I realize that a few dozen pizzas could never truly repay the debt that we owe them. They were very caring people and always looked out for Sharon. I will never forget one of the techs, Rashid, in his heavy Moroccan accent, telling everyone, "Take good care of her—she's my sister." I always marveled at the sensitive caring manner in which everyone dealt with Sharon.

As a patient it can often be frightening when you are about to be lifted or transferred. There is often a little voice in your head expressing concern, hoping that they don't drop you. Another tech, Fred, had a unique way of getting Sharon from her bed to her wheelchair. He would always say, "It's time for our dance," and he would hold Sharon as if they were going to dance, lift her straight up, and pivot her around. Before she knew it, she was in the wheelchair.

As Sharon got stronger, she began to transfer in and out of her bed and wheelchair on her own and didn't need to "dance" anymore. But she needed to be careful, as fatigue is an ever-present factor with GBS, and fatigue can lead to loss of balance and falls.

Sometimes Sharon would sleep so soundly that it was difficult to wake her. One morning Doctor Kraus was making rounds and, try as he might, could not rouse her. Finally he said, "You know you're going home today, don't you?" Her eyes sprung open instantly to see Doctor Kraus chuckling. Of course he was only joking and she knew it, but it was effective in waking her up.

The truth was that while Sharon was not going home that day, we were in fact very close to the point where the team would begin to discuss a discharge date, and we were full of anticipation. I thought about everything that we had gone through in the previous months and began to feel a sense of relief as I looked at Sharon's progress.

The heavy burden that had been weighing down on us for months was gradually lifting. Sharon's life was no longer in danger; she was free of the ventilator and was getting stronger every day. She could communicate by simply speaking, not needing to use the board with the letters on it. She could eat real food and enjoy it. My daily trips to the hospital were a relaxing ride in the country, not a death-defying mission on Interstate 95 into the city.

Most of all, with each day came the belief that the goal for Sharon to walk out of the hospital would become reality. I was sure of it, and I wanted everyone to know. On Sunday, August 20, I e-mailed the following to our "Prayer Warriors":

Good evening,

As I look at the date, it's hard to believe that summer is almost over.

Sharon continues to get stronger and show off her daily increases in strength. Yesterday *she walked!* She went four steps in the parallel bars. She's very excited. One of her fears was that she might come home in a wheelchair, but this experience has provided hope and determination to leave the hospital on her feet. In fact, she has set a goal to keep a commitment we have for the second weekend of October that will involve some traveling. Ambitious? Yes! One thing we have learned, however, is that it is important when setting any goal to *put a date on it!* Otherwise, it's just a wish. Once you've put a date on it, you've committed yourself to it.

We had maintained belief, that belief had given results, and I was confident that those results would create more belief for Sharon. I was ecstatic about Sharon taking her first steps. I knew that four steps would become eight and then forty and then eighty. I knew because I too had gone through the process of learning to walk again. It was always uplifting to see Sharon doing something that she wasn't able to do the day before.

She was reaching the point that I promised her she would when her gains would become exponential. Her progress, which began as baby steps, was coming in leaps and bounds.

And I had enough belief that I was willing to put it in writing.

I must say that Sharon did a far better job learning to walk again than I did. I spent a fair amount of time hitting the floor. Sharon was more cautious than I was. There was one fellow who worked as an assistant in therapy to whom Sharon referred to as "pillow boy." Sharon told him one day that his job was to throw himself on the ground and act as a pillow to break her fall should she ever go down while trying to walk! He was agreeable to that but promised that he would never let her fall, a promise that was kept.

One of the many things that Bryn Mawr Rehab made available for the patients was equestrian therapy. Working to maintain balance on the horse is very effective at strengthening one's trunk muscles. Thorncroft Stables is right around the corner from the hospital, and Sharon had several opportunities to take part in riding. She had never been on a horse in her life so naturally was a little apprehensive. The folks at Thorncroft could not have been any nicer or any more accommodating. They have a ramp so the patients in wheelchairs can get right next to the horse and slide over onto its back. They do a fabulous job of working to make the patients feel comfortable.

Each time that she went, Sharon rode the most beautiful horse named Libby, a gentle and majestic animal. Sharon loved riding Libby and was looking forward to her next visit. I was happy to be able to be part of the experience as I felt that it was important for me to be with Sharon as much as possible as she went through each step in her rehabilitation process.

Within a week, Sharon had progressed to the point where she was making several passes at a time through the parallel bars and then started using a walker. She was really cute because she got to the point where she didn't want anybody telling me what had gone on if I had not been there to see it. Sharon wanted to tell me herself. It just tickled me to no end to walk in, see her grinning, and have her say to me, "Guess what I did?"

Once again, the hospital was buzzing with excitement. Her accomplishments were good for everybody. The therapists and the nurses are always happy to see the results of their efforts, and such events often served as inspiration to other patients who might have been struggling with their own fears and doubts.

Sharon and I continued to give thanks for all that God had blessed us with. Every night before I would leave the hospital, Sharon, Ann, and I would hold hands and pray for perpetual strength and blessings. Sharon was making such great progress, and we were surrounded by so many great people. Sharon had become an inspiration to so many people as they watched her being transformed. She had arrived there on a stretcher with little motor activity and was going to walk out when it came time to leave.

Little by little, patients and their families would seek us out. I'm not sure why, but looking back I think it was mostly out of curiosity. I just don't think that any of them knew what to make of us. There we were, going through a tragic period in our lives, and we just didn't let the pain show. I would come in as if I owned the place, always smiling and giving the nurses a high-five or a hug. Sharon was always upbeat despite all of the challenges that she faced.

And we were always laughing and trying to have a good time. I think that people must have thought, *We want whatever they have!*

One night Sharon and I were sitting out on the back patio, and two ladies approached us. They were sisters (kin sisters, not nun sisters) and were there visiting their father who had suffered a stroke. These two ladies were visibly distraught over their father's situation, as one would expect, and began talking with Sharon and me. They asked what had happened to us. Our story usually makes people's jaws hit the ground. After explaining that my injury occurred many years ago and that Sharon had been stricken with GBS, they asked straight out how we dealt with all of it. I told them that we simply take one day at a time. I explained that every night we would give thanks to God for carrying us through another day, and each morning we would ask God for the wisdom, strength, and courage to do what we had to do *that* day. That's it. Don't worry about tomorrow and remember that yesterday is history. Take each day one by one and have faith in God.

A few nights later I had the chance to meet their father down at the pond. There was a pond on the premises that had fish and some really large snapping turtles in it. We used to get crackers from the nurses' station, and I would wheel Sharon down to the pond so she could get exercise throwing the crackers to the turtles. We're talking about some really big turtles here. Let me tell you something, it doesn't take much to amuse us, and you just can't get this kind of entertainment in the city! Sharon loves being outdoors, and after all of the months she spent in a hospital bed, she really looked forward to sitting by the pond in the evenings. So anyway, we were feeding the turtles when those two ladies came down with their father in his wheelchair, so we had the opportunity to speak with him and their mother. I hope that we were able to be of some comfort to them. While I lost touch and don't know how well he recovered, I keep him on my daily prayer list. They were really nice folks.

I got to the point where I had to start writing down all of the people we were praying for, as my memory is not always good when it comes to names. So I started carrying a list with me, and every night when we would say our prayers, in addition to praying for us, we would pray for all of those on our list. Needless to say, the list has grown quite a bit over the last few years.

———

Sharon remained as a great source of inspiration for other patients as she worked on getting stronger and walked greater distances. But we were approaching the time when she would be discharged, and the cold hard truth was that her ankles just weren't strong enough for her to safely walk any great distance. Sharon was going to have to wear braces just like I do. I know firsthand just how uncomfortable they are, and I think that I was more bothered by the idea than she was. But Sharon simply took it in stride.

Molds were taken of her legs, and within a few days she had the new braces. There was an instant change in her ability to walk, as she was much more stable. She began working on walking up and down ramps as well as steps. She was also able to cover greater distances, which meant that we really had to keep an eye on her. Giving someone new leg braces is almost like giving a new teen driver car keys—they want to go everywhere!

We also needed to work on her ability to get in and out of a vehicle safely, so on the scheduled day I made sure I brought our truck to the hospital—no sense in making it easy for her. The first time Sharon climbed into the truck, she closed the door and wasn't coming out. It was another one of those precious moments, as she was ready to leave. It took a little bit of effort to coax her out of the truck. She really wanted to go home right then, and it was tough convincing her that it would just be a few more days.

We had been given a tentative discharge date, and neither one of us could wait. Although I saw Sharon every day, I had been living alone for almost five months and didn't like it very much. Sharon missed the daily routine she once knew. She missed working in her flower gardens. I missed all of the things that we used to do together. I missed saying goodnight and awakening the next morning to find her next to me. I missed all of the silly things that she would always do that made us laugh so hard. Time would be more manageable, as I wouldn't be going to the hospital every day. We just had to be patient a little while longer.

Now that isn't to say that Sharon didn't do any silly things at all while she was in the hospital. One day she was in the gym using a particular piece of equipment that was for the purpose of building strength in her arms. They called it the rickshaw because of one's position while using it. The idea is to push down on the two handles against the resistance of weights, the amount of which is determined by the therapist.

Well, wouldn't you know it, there was Sharon trying to show me how well she was doing but doing it all wrong. Instead of pushing down, she was pulling up and lifting the whole machine up off the floor! It was a priceless moment. And I think it was safe to say that she was getting stronger, as this machine probably weighed several hundred pounds.

Sharon spent the last week working with Megan, Kristin, and Joann perfecting everything that she had learned, kind of like a tune-up practice before the big game. They were glad that Sharon was going to be discharged shortly, but it was obvious that they would miss her dearly. They had worked so very hard and had taken such a personal interest in Sharon that I knew there was a sentimental moment on the horizon.

Early on the morning of September 19, Doctor Kraus came into Sharon's room and awakened her. It would be his last official morning rounds with Sharon. When she awoke he said, "You're going home today, but we have one small problem. Everybody likes you and Bob, so if you're leaving, he has to stay." I can honestly say that his words were probably the highest compliment we have ever received from anyone. We had all developed very good working, as well as personal, relationships. These people were just so very good to Sharon.

That morning was a tearful time for many. These people had really taken a liking to Sharon—who wouldn't? So many of them often commented on how Sharon was so easy to take care of. Sharon is a sweet lady, the type of person that everyone wants to be around. They were going to miss her, and we were going to miss them. But it was time to move on. That, of course, was easier said than done, as I too had grown so fond of everyone there.

As I signed all of the paperwork regarding Sharon's discharge, Fred came over to say good-bye. Sharon said to Fred, "How about one more dance?" She stood up and gave Fred a big hug. He was such a gentle soul and had taken such good care of her. I put all of the paperwork in my briefcase, and we left the Spruce Unit with one of the nurses, who pushed Sharon in her wheelchair. As we passed the nurses' station, I removed my "I Love Nurses" and "Nurses Rock!" badges, ceremoniously hung them on their bulletin board, and said good-bye.

When we approached the front doors of the hospital, I asked the nurse to stop. Sharon *needed* to walk out through those doors. The nurse protested slightly, explaining to me about hospital policy and how patients must be wheeled to the vehicle. I protested a little bit myself and explained the goal that had been set and how important it was for Sharon to walk out of the hospital. I understood about policy, and I knew that this gal really cared, as she was one of the team that had been so protective of Sharon. Finally, she gave in by simply saying, "Just don't get me in trouble."

I handed Sharon her walker; she carefully stood up from the wheelchair, walked out through the front doors with me, pausing only briefly for a picture, and then continued walking to where the truck was parked. She climbed up into the truck and closed the door. After five months and four hospitals, my bride was finally coming home. We had prayed for this day, and God was listening.

Rebuilding Again

I took the long way home so Sharon could enjoy some of the scenery that she hadn't seen in five months. I was happy that Sharon was finally coming home, but it felt strange at the same time. There I was, driving down the road on my way home from the hospital, and she was in the seat right next to me. That seat had been empty for five months.

While I, in my own naïve way, thought that time would be more manageable once Sharon came home, the fact was that time would become a bigger issue. Now I would be taking care of her twenty-four hours a day. Don't misread this and think of it as a complaint—it's not. Granted, Sharon was able to do a lot for herself by this point. But I had spent the previous five months worrying about and watching over her, and it is not something that one can simply flip a switch and turn off. Admittedly, I was probably placing more of a burden on myself than was necessary. After all, Sharon was getting better. But I was still worried about her. And during those five months, there were trained professionals caring for her around the clock, and we were not allowed to bring any of them home with us. However, a few of the younger nurses did ask us if we would like to adopt them. That would have kept the neighbors talking!

Sharon still had a lot of ground to cover and was going to need time to make her own adjustments to being home. It had been difficult for me to adjust when I got out of the hospital years ago, but I lived alone. If I had a tough time, I only had myself to deal with.

Sharon was in the process of adapting to what had been and what would continue to be a series of life changing events. I had been through the rebuilding process myself, and now it was Sharon's turn. It was important that I give her space and time to deal with things at her pace but still be there to help and support her.

Truth be told, I was afraid of what the future might hold for us. Would both of us be strong enough to deal with the changes happening? Would I be accepting of all of the changes? Did I really have what it would take to be the husband that Sharon now needed me to be? I didn't know the answers and was afraid of what the answers might be. I would only find out in time. Perhaps I took the long way home for many reasons.

We stopped at the day care center on the way home in order for Sharon to visit with staff briefly. In addition to Sharon wanting to see everyone, it was also important that they see that she really was coming back. We had done a very good job of keeping her absence quiet. Between summer vacations and schedule changes, it was actually somewhere near the end of August before clients started noticing that they hadn't seen Sharon for a while. By that point, having a tentative discharge date, we were able to tell them that she had been sick and that they could expect to see her in a few weeks.

It was interesting to observe the reactions from the different children. A few of the older children simply took in stride that Sharon was back. Many noticed the very subtle physical changes right away and asked all of the typical questions that one would expect kids to ask. Children are curious by nature and are often more observant than we give them credit for.

There is rarely a week that goes by that, while out in public, I don't have a small child ask me why I'm different. I always find it amusing to watch the reaction of the parents, usually being one of embarrassment. I assure them that it is all right for the child to ask, and I take the time to talk to the child about what happened to me and to explain that we are all different from one another in many ways. It never bothers me when children ask such questions, and I actually see it as a positive sign that they are observant of what is around them.

There was one little girl, Samantha, who had been in the baby room at the time Sharon got sick. Samantha had taken a shine to both Sharon and me and had become our best buddy. At less than two years of age, not seeing someone for five months pretty much makes them a stranger. Samantha had the strangest look on her face the first time she saw Sharon, and we could only imagine what she was thinking. It was sort of a cross between, *I know you from somewhere, but I'm not sure,* and, *Hey, I thought you were my buddy—where have you been?* She has since gotten reacquainted and has become just a little possessive of Sharon and me.

Although Sharon was in no way ready to go back to her old schedule yet, we made a point of her being there most days for an hour or so at the end of the day near pickup time. I felt that it was important for clients to see her there, as her presence was important to everyone. We kept the schedule and pace light, as Sharon became fatigued very easily. We didn't want to do anything that would risk any setbacks or injuries. Sharon was finally home, and I didn't want to be apart from her again. I remember the first night that she was home all I could do was hold her. Well, I held her and cried a few tears of joy. Sharon is, and had always been, my reason to get up every day. I had come so close to losing the best gift I had ever received. I held Sharon, my precious love, closer than ever.

I shared all of my feelings and fears with Sharon. We still had so much ahead of us, both with Sharon's recovery and as husband and wife. We quickly realized that all we really needed to do was to continue what we had done so far—have faith in God, pray for strength, take one day at a time, be there for each other no matter what, and not quit. And I would make it a priority to oversee her therapy and work with her each day.

———

The insurance company had contracted with therapists and a nurse to come out to the house to work with Sharon temporarily until we arranged for outpatient therapy. The wheels of progress are often slow, and it was well over a month before we were able to make all of the arrangements. One of our concerns, in addition to improving her ambulation, was finding someone to work with Sharon's hands, as they were very weak and had limited range of motion. The months of paralysis had taken their toll on her hands, and despite my best efforts at range of motion exercises, the muscles had extensive atrophy.

After visiting and interviewing several facilities, we found a therapy facility locally that had a hand specialist on site. We quickly got Sharon scheduled, and she began doing two sessions of physical therapy and two sessions with the hand specialist each week. Sharon's progress was steady, but it was still important to watch her fatigue level. In addition to the two days each week at therapy, she continued to work every day on her own using weights and elastic bands. She was pushing hard to make the maximum progress that was possible, as she wanted desperately to get to the point where she would no longer need to wear the leg braces. Sharon was grateful to have them, but they are not very comfortable to wear—I know, as I am approaching two decades of wearing them.

As several months passed, Sharon's strength and balance improved, and she began to walk using only one cane instead of two. I do not believe that I have ever met a more determined person in my life than Sharon. A lot of folks would have given up by this point. In one of our many conversations about her illness, Sharon recalled the night she was flown downtown from the local hospital. She recalled how she knew deep in her heart that this was going to be a very long process and that her attitude would have to carry her. She had, and continues to have, the strength of twenty people.

By the middle of February 2007, Sharon had used the total amount of visits for therapy as allowed by the insurance company. Despite having documentation from doctors indicating the need for more therapy, a request for an extension was denied as well as the appeal we filed against the insurance company's denial. But in looking at what the insurance company had spent to date, we really were not in a position to complain. And it actually worked out for the best.

Fortunately the facility that Sharon had been using offered a program where, for a monthly fee, she could continue to use the equipment. Under this program, Sharon would not have a therapist working with her but, by this point, knew what she needed to do. Needless to say we jumped at the opportunity, and Sharon continued her therapy regiment two times a week using the weight machines, in addition to her daily exercises at home. The silver lining was that the monthly fee ended up being far less than the co-pays being spent while going to therapy.

I remained involved and monitored Sharon's progress. I was beginning to feel confident that she just might be able to discontinue wearing the leg braces. I don't recall the exact date, but sometime in April 2007 Sharon asked me how she would know when she was able to go without them, as nobody was following her case at that point. Judging by the speed at which Sharon was getting around, I had no doubts at all that she was ready. I simply told her to take the braces off and try going without them but to use her cane and to be careful! There was no looking back as Sharon has never worn the braces since.

Fortunately, Sharon has only fallen a few times, fewer times than I fall on a weekly basis!

While we were hoping and praying for a complete recovery, it doesn't appear as if that is to become reality. I persist in praying and asking God that Sharon will become completely well, if it is His will. Sharon still has some weakness and a lack of sensation in her legs and feet, as well as in her hands, which makes a lot of daily tasks challenging. While the muscles in the right side of her face have improved, they have not recovered fully, leaving Sharon with weakness (she claims that she smiles like Popeye) and some difficulty with vision in her right eye.

Despite all of the changes that have occurred, I believe that our relationship, as well as our faith in God, has grown stronger. We both feel truly blessed that we have been able to maintain our belief in one another. Years ago when I was recovering from my accident, I recall being told of how so many marriages end in divorce and how relationships change after a severe injury or illness. While I have never seen actual statistics, the numbers were supposedly pretty high. That thought kept replaying in my mind as I wondered what the future would hold for us. Fortunately, we both have been strong enough to accept all of the changes. All of the worries that I had I have been able to put aside. Of course Sharon, being the rock that she is, was never worried.

I do not believe that any person can experience a major event and not come through it changed in some way. As we go through life, our experiences, whether good or bad, help to shape and mold who we are. But I also believe that while our background and experiences may affect who we are, we are ultimately responsible for who we become, thus stressing the importance of having a good moral foundation and the ability to think.

We all have a choice in regard to how we react to things, as God has given each of us a free will that enables us to make those choices.

Sharon and I simply choose to decide that we will not quit. We will not quit on each other or anything that we do. Now I'm not saying that either one of us hasn't had a day where we might have thought, *How much more can I take?* And I'm not saying that there has never been a time when the idea of quitting something might start to creep in just a little. After all, we are human. But we have a rule that says we're just not allowed to both quit on the same day. That way there is always one of us to give the other a boot in the behind and say, "Snap out of it!" It has worked so far. Besides, as we are both now handicapped, it takes the two of us to do what one person would normally do. We are quite a pair.

As time has moved on, we have talked more and more about the period in which Sharon was hospitalized. I never really pushed hard, as I knew that Sharon would talk about things as she became comfortable. Sharon obviously had her fears, but then who wouldn't? However, interestingly enough, she has said repeatedly that there was never a time when she thought that she was going to die.

There are a few things that Sharon has not talked about at any length up to this point.

The hospital environment, coupled with some of the drugs that are administered, can sometimes make for a frightening time to say the least. While Sharon has only touched on those situations briefly, she pretty much summed it up by saying that she will never understand how people could intentionally take hallucinogens in the sixties. Enough said.

Sharon was fully aware of her surroundings and of everything going on during the duration of her illness. For months, everything except for her attitude was out of her control as she lay motionless. When I asked how she dealt with it all, Sharon told me that she would just pray to God for a sense of peace and maintain the belief that she was going to get better. She is a very patient and determined woman. Sharon would also mentally take herself to the one place she loves the most—the beach.

I have mentioned how one of the compact discs that I would play was a soundtrack of ocean waves crashing and seagulls. It helped Sharon transport herself to her favorite location. By October 2007, thirteen months after being discharged from the hospital, Sharon felt well enough to travel and was able to enjoy a week in sunny Florida. She thoroughly enjoyed feeling the warm sun on her while listening to a real ocean and real seagulls. She was truly at peace. And all I got was a lousy T-shirt! Just kidding, I was at peace too.

It did my heart good to see her finally at peace, as Sharon is my life. Time has helped to ease the pain that I felt as I watched her struggle for so many months, although I will never forget it. A sense of guilt had gnawed at me now and then, as I wondered if I could have or should have done more. During the first few weeks of Sharon's illness, I had serious doubts about whether she would survive. We had lost twenty-four valuable hours at a local facility. The doctors were telling me one thing, and my instincts were telling me another. Unfortunately, my instincts were correct. It was one of those times where I would have welcomed being wrong. Could I have done more? Should I have transferred Sharon sooner? Sharon and I have talked about this at length, and she has assured me that she is comfortable with all of the decisions that I made. And the fact is, it is history. I have had to let go of it. But I'm a little smarter for it.

It has taken me awhile to finally realize that we

can't change the past, that we simply need to move forward. We can't rewrite history, but we need to remember what we learn from it. Sharon and I continue to take one day at a time, and we continue building our love for one another. And we remain thankful to God every day for the blessings we have received.

A Few Things We Have Learned Along the Way

It's been quite a ride so far. And despite everything that has happened, I still believe that it has been a good ride. Like most people, Sharon and I have had a vast number of experiences in our lives, some good and some—well—not so good. There definitely have been a few twists in the road. But along the way, and throughout all of these experiences, there have been many lessons. If we were to ignore those lessons, or even worse, be unaware of them, then we would be missing out completely. It would mean that our experiences were for nothing.

While many of the important things that we have learned have been a result of our experiences, we have been fortunate enough to learn from others, mentors who have gone down the road ahead of us and who know where the bumpy spots can be.

And so I want to share a few ideas with you. I don't think that it would be enough to share with you our experiences and not share with you what they all mean. So, here goes.

Life Isn't Always Easy, and It Isn't Always Fair

Life isn't always easy, and it isn't always fair. And we need to just learn to accept it. I'll admit that was pretty blunt, wasn't it? But you know something? I don't recall ever having anyone promise that life would be easy or fair.

Nearly all of us have heard of "Murphy's law." Now I must confess that I haven't the first clue about who this Murphy character is, and I certainly wish he would keep his law to himself! However, the fact is that things can and will go wrong. It's inevitable.

And there is another bitter pill that we sometimes must swallow, that being the realization that sometimes situations that seem unfair or difficult end up being the result of decisions or choices that we have made, a lesson I have learned all too often. And then, oftentimes, we want to point the finger at someone else and say, "But it wasn't my fault."

Personal responsibility seems to be a lost art anymore. It's too easy to place blame elsewhere and not face the guy or gal in the mirror. During a few points in my life, I went through some significantly rough times, and I faced a few demons along the way.

I swore up and down that it wasn't my fault and that it was everybody else's. And it was the circumstances. I was too busy pointing the finger at everyone else, so I didn't notice that while doing it, I had several fingers pointing right back at me. I needed to get a new attitude; I needed a check-up from the neck up! And God was watching. He sent me some situations and some problems to solve that forced me to make some choices. And as a result, I was able to put things in perspective and accept things for what they were.

Over the years Sharon and I have learned that the sooner we accept the fact that life isn't always fair, the easier it is to deal with life. We all need to learn to roll with the punches. Now of course the pharmaceutical companies and the legal community would have you believe otherwise. We have become a society that seeks financial compensation for every little inconvenience. You slipped and fell? Blame somebody, and no doubt you can receive a financial windfall. Minor fender bender? Wear a foam collar for a while to convince a jury that you are hurt. You will get something.

From time to time we have been asked if we took any legal action, given how Sharon's case was handled in the beginning. The topic of medical liability is one that goes far beyond the scope of this book, but the answer, simply, is that we did not pursue anything. While it is our belief that people should be held accountable if harm is done, it leads us to the question of just what exactly constitutes accountability. Acknowledging the error? Saying they are sorry? Mending their ways? Or perhaps having their insurance carrier write a check? But is anybody really being accountable?

The fact is that a big fat check won't change what happened or cause Sharon to be healed 100%. And we don't believe that it would cause certain parties to suddenly develop compassion. Besides, neither one of us likes swimming with sharks; it's just not our idea of a good time. I'd rather have my teeth drilled without Novocain. Perhaps taking some folks out behind the barn and just giving them a good old fashioned whoopin' would make a difference. But then, maybe it wouldn't. Unfortunately, the fact remains that sometimes bad things just happen. Life is full of inconveniences, and unfortunately, too many people try to turn an event of misfortune or sadness into a payday.

And if things do not go their way, there is always medication. I recently saw an ad in the newspaper looking for participants for a *clinical research study using an investigative drug* for sad people. The ad asked the following four questions. Do you feel depressed? Do you have trouble concentrating? Are you less interested in things you used to enjoy? Do you feel tired or without energy?

If you answered yes to any or all of those questions, you could obtain study medication, study related care, and, hold on to your seats, folks—reimbursement for your time! Now I truly do not mean to sound as if I am poking fun at sad people. I'm not, honest. But truthfully, how many of us have felt a little down at some point? Trouble concentrating? Some days I could be the poster child. We all lose interest in various activities, and given the schedules many people keep, of course they may lack energy or get tired. It's called life!

Every one of us has stuff happen to us on a daily basis. Things are going to happen to us all that are inconvenient, sometimes painful, and that we have no control over. The one thing that we do have control over is how we react to it. Sharon often says that her grandmother used to tell her, "There's no point getting mad, because you just have to get glad again." Amen.

When Sharon's condition first plummeted and we were waiting for the helicopter to transfer her, one of the doctors asked me if I needed anything in the way of some pharmaceutical help (my words, not his) to get through the ordeal. Thanks, but no thanks, doc. My faith would carry me. Although I'm not saying that it was easy. I know that the doctor meant well, but that was the last thing I needed or wanted. I never would have asked for such a thing on my own. Yes, I was terrified of what was ahead. Yes, my head was full of thoughts such as, *Why is this happening to us?* or, *Is Sharon going to die?* And believe me, there wasn't anything about that situation that was fair. That's the way it goes some days.

But, again, we all have a choice as to how we will react to things. We are all, for the most part, where we choose to be. We have a choice every day as to whether we are going to make it a good day or a bad day. We can either stay in the game or park it on the bench because the game isn't going our way. Sharon and I think that staying in the game is a great idea.

Keep Things in Perspective

There is an old Irish prayer that my father used to repeatedly tell me:

> *God, grant me the serenity to accept the things I can-*
> *not change, the courage to change the things I*
> *can, and the wisdom to know the difference.*

That prayer has served me well throughout my life, particularly in the last few years. I know full well how easily one can become overwhelmed with circumstances. But we have to know the difference between what we can and cannot change.

One of the key words in the last phrase of the prayer is *wisdom*. How do we acquire wisdom? When I hear that word, it is easy to envision a group of wise men or great thinkers—people who possess high IQs and great amounts of knowledge, who, well, I guess they think a lot of great thoughts. Nothing could be further from the truth.

The dictionary defines *wisdom* as "knowledge and good judgment based on experience."[1] So from this it is rather evident that wisdom has very little to do with thinking great thoughts or how high of an IQ we may or may not have. We gain wisdom by living life and experiencing as many things as we can. Now, like in many facets of life, there is a catch. We gain knowledge and good judgment through experience, but as I have found all too often, the experiences that we learn from the most are the ones that were often a result of *bad* judgment.

For example, when I was a teenager, I learned several of the laws of physics through the improper operation of an automobile. I learned about things like gravity and momentum and how those forces act upon an automobile once you actually get it airborne.

Talk about a scary ride! Don't try this at home either, and don't ask me what I was thinking. I did, however, walk away from the episode with wisdom because I learned something and vowed to forever use good judgment based on that experience. I also had to walk several hundred yards to go pick up the battery that had fallen out of the car, bring it back, and put it in so I could drive out of there.

But I learned a lot of things that day. One should not drive their sister's car fast enough to get airborne, or any car, for that matter. But if one is so inclined, a change of laundry is a swell idea. There are some things that just have to be learned firsthand. My sister Maryanne gained wisdom too (and a new battery courtesy of my stupidity) and didn't let me drive her car anymore.

All of the things that we do and things that we experience shape who we are and how we think. The episode involving the car was something that I had control over but chose to be stupid about. But I hope we learn not to repeat mistakes and learn what things we can and cannot control. I believe that even positive experiences have lessons that we can take from them. And sometimes the lessons are not from our experiences but from the experiences of those wiser than us.

But above all, we need to avoid playing what I refer to as the "what if" game. All too often, we can become preoccupied with things that haven't even happened yet or may never happen for that matter. I have often been as guilty of this as the next person.

When Sharon was in the hospital, occasionally random thoughts would creep into my head, and I would say, *"What if* Sharon doesn't survive this? What am I going to do?" Well, I wasn't going to do anything about it because Sharon was determined to survive. And she did. And most of it was out of my control anyway. Generally speaking, most of what falls into the "what if" category is going to be out of our control. So let it go.

It was that little prayer that helped me to keep my sanity while I was recovering from my accident and while Sharon was going through her illness. Sharon and I have learned to just focus on those things that we can control. Time and energy spent worrying about what might happen or what could have happened is time and energy wasted.

Don't mistake these thoughts as to mean that one should just be nonchalant about everything or that one should not have a contingency plan of action. Quite the contrary.

I was never nonchalant regarding Sharon's condition or her care. But I couldn't afford to fall apart at the seams, for my sake and for hers. And I was always thinking ahead about the next thing that might have to be done regarding her care. There was absolutely no way that I had any control over Sharon's illness. But I had control over her care and her surroundings.

When the first treatment team dropped the ball and Sharon almost died, I had a choice—take an anti-depressant or take action. I chose to take control of the things that I had control over. And the only thing I could control at that point was who would be treating her. So Ann and I moved Sharon to a hospital that would take her case seriously and not tell me that it was not a big deal. And then once again, it was out of my hands. The only thing I had control over was formulating a plan for her care and remaining involved. I could not, however, control the outcome. That is the difference between planning ahead and worrying ahead.

Years ago when I was working toward my instrument rating, my flight instructor introduced me to an interesting concept. One day while we were flying, he asked me what the two most important things were when flying on instruments in bad weather.

I immediately began searching for the right answer: "Airspeed? Altitude? Heading? Communication? Why are you asking me this stupid question when I'm flying in the clouds trying to keep this plane upright?"

He said that the two most important things are the next two things that you will have to do. That was his way of saying to think ahead and stay ahead of the airplane. He said to *think* ahead. He never mentioned a thing about *worrying* ahead. If the weather is bad at the destination airport, you can't afford to worry about it and lose control. You simply choose your alternate airport, which, of course, you planned ahead for.

So try to apply all of these things to everyday life. Keep things in perspective. Rely on wisdom from past experiences to know what you have control over and what you don't have control over. There have certainly been times when I have expected the worst only to have things turn out fine. And then I would ask myself why I was so worried. Take control over that which we can. Those things that we can't control—say a prayer and put them in God's hands.

Dream Big and Don't Quit

There have been countless books written about attitude, perseverance, and the importance of having a dream, and over the years I have read plenty of them. I am telling you firsthand that Sharon and I are living proof of the importance of a positive attitude and setting one's goals high. Intelligence, talent, good looks, education—none of these can take the place of attitude.

After all, Sharon is intelligent, educated, talented, and by far one great-looking lady.

But none of those qualities could save her when she became ill. And while I long to have those qualities that Sharon possesses (except the part about being a great-looking lady—I fall out of heels), the fact is that those qualities wouldn't have made the slightest difference when I was trying to walk again. When we were going through our respective challenges, we each simply made the decision that we were going to accomplish the goal that we had set.

Yes, it is true that neither one of us made a full

recovery. But we accomplished what we did by having a big dream and by putting a date on it. Set the goals high and make the commitment. Otherwise, it's only a wish. It would have been easy for either of us to say, "I hope to walk someday." Or in Sharon's case, even worse, she could have said, "Gee, maybe someday I'll be off of the ventilator and breathing on my own." *Someday* never comes. Take that word out of your vocabulary! Give yourself a deadline to meet.

Sure, sometimes we don't always meet our deadlines, but it's something to shoot for. And if we miss, that's what new deadlines are for. But don't give up. Just keep taking one more step.

Don't worry if someone else thinks that your goal is too high or is unreasonable. It's your goal, not theirs. Too many people worry about what others will think, sometimes even worrying about their friends. I can only say that I do not care at all what a stranger thinks, and if a friend is being critical of a goal that I am striving for, then they are not my friend. If I had listened to many of those around me, I never would have stood or walked again. And if Sharon had not set her goals high, she would not have walked out of the hospital.

I was once given some great advice, that if something seems impossible, just add an apostrophe to the word *impossible* and it becomes *I'm possible*. If I believe in myself, then *I'm possible,* and I can accomplish whatever I want to. Sharon and I apply this to whatever challenge we encounter. In the end, it doesn't matter what anyone else thinks. We all need to run our own race. Ultimately, we only have to answer to two people—God and that person that we see in the mirror.

Give Thanks Every Day

What a concept! Give thanks every day. I have often said this to people only to have them ask, "For what?" Hmm, well, let me think. How about giving thanks for everything we have? If we all were to make a list, we would realize just how many blessings we all have. Most people are better off than they realize, although some do not see it because they have become focused on any problems they are facing.

And speaking of problems, give thanks for those too. Say what? Yes, that's what I said; we should give thanks for the problems that we face. Why? Well, because we are dealing with the problems we have and not the problems that someone else has. Again, I go back to when I was in the hospital in the body cast. Initially I was feeling sorry for myself. Actually, I was being a big baby. That was until I looked around at other patients and saw how well-off I was. I gave thanks. I gave *a lot* of thanks.

I am not trying to diminish anything that people might be going through. But what Sharon and I have learned is that God's blessings are abundant. Sharon and I both have permanent medical issues, but we try to always focus on the positive things. Any time we have hit an obstacle in life, we have been able to resolve it with God's help.

Giving thanks daily enables us to keep in mind just how blessed we are. We also take the time to ask God to bless those that are in need. Over the last few years, we have accumulated quite a list of people that we pray for daily. We find that by praying for others, we become less focused on our own challenges. Giving thanks makes it much easier to see the glass as half full instead of half empty.

Ask for Help

I once saw a sign in a man's office that read, *If I had to do it over, I would ask for help.* Profound words, huh? I thought so, because I could really relate to them. Throughout most of my life, I have never been one to rely on others for help. I always had the I-can-do-it-myself attitude. It was never some kind of tough-guy macho thing. I simply have always been pretty much of a loner and have kept most things close to the vest.

Added to that is that my personality is such that I always have a certain way of doing things, a certain order. I swear it's a curse. Jack often teases me and refers to it as "the Captain Bob sense of order" (at least I think he's teasing), a place for everything and everything in its place. As a result, I never got very good at delegating or asking for help. After all, if you want something done properly, you have do it yourself, right? Wrong! Sometimes you have no choice but to enlist the help of others. And sometimes that means stepping out on faith and trusting others.

Change is a funny thing, as it is not something that most people embrace. It can be uncomfortable. In fact, it can be downright painful at times. But I can tell you that when the pain of staying the same becomes greater than the pain of changing, you'll change!

We all need to know our limitations, and over the past few years, I have come to accept mine. A little gentle nudge from Sharon now and then has helped me learn that it really is okay to ask for help.

When Sharon was stricken with the GBS, I knew immediately that I was in way over my head. I was taking the express lane out of my comfort zone and had no choice but to change my way of thinking and rely on others. Ann and I became a team and worked together to make sure things got done. It was an education in planning, communicating, and teamwork, something I definitely was not accustomed to. The only planning and communicating that I had ever been familiar with was in flying. Other than that, I was lone man out for most of my life.

A little bit of teamwork turned out to be a rewarding experience in many ways. For one thing, we accomplished the mission at hand—taking care of Sharon. It gave me the opportunity to rely on my strengths and to acknowledge my weaknesses. And in acknowledging those weaknesses, I had the opportunity to rely on the strengths of someone else, and in doing so I gained a little wisdom in the process.

I learned that it is a sign of strength and wisdom to ask for help and that people really will rise to the occasion, step in, and help to carry the load. Asking someone for their help signifies that you trust them. And the bigger the problem, the greater the help that is required, and so a greater degree of trust is needed. It is probably the greatest compliment one can pay to another.

Tomorrow Is a Gift

Many times I have heard people say that tomorrow is a gift, and I never really gave it much thought. Although, the one thing that has crossed my mind over the years is how much I dislike clichés. That was up until the two times in my life that tomorrow almost didn't happen.

In the hectic, fast-paced, and complicated world in which we all live, it is actually quite easy to take time and people for granted. I know that I certainly did. When I refer to my taking people for granted, I don't mean that in the sense of taking advantage of people, although that does happen in life. I simply mean that, at least in my case, I took for granted that people would always be there.

I believed that tomorrow would always be there. The sun will rise tomorrow just as it did today. Or will it? And even if it does, will I be here to see it? Will all of those dear to me be here to see it? I feel that it has become easy to forget the value of people and time.

We live in what I refer to as a "disposable" world. We don't fix things anymore. If the television breaks, it hits the curb on trash day, and we buy a new one.

It is commonplace to trade automobiles long before there is any significant wear on them. Nothing needs to be built to last, since we probably won't keep it long anyway. And chances are that things won't be taken care of as well since they don't need to last. Is it possible that we sometimes view time and relationships in the same light? Could be. When I look at each new day that we are given and the people that surround us, I see gifts. I see gifts that we can take care of and treasure, or we can just take them for granted and use them until they break or wear out.

A man once posed a very interesting question to me. He asked, "If tomorrow was the last day of your life and I wanted to buy it from you, how much would you charge me?"

I really had to think long and hard on that one. I was truly perplexed, trying to imagine what a day of life would be worth. Finally the man asked, "How about whatever it was that you sold today for?" That question really caused me to think about just how we can squander time and take those around us for granted. Well, no more.

Make a Difference

I recall once walking into my father's office as a young lad and overhearing an audiotape he had playing. I could not even begin to tell you who the man speaking was, but I recall his words. He said to treat every person you meet as if they are the most important person in the world.

Remembering those words both amazes and concerns me. For some reason those words have stuck with me for all of these years. But what concerns me is that despite remembering the words so clearly, I haven't always been the person that I need to be when it comes to how others should be treated. And as such, this has given me cause for great reflection.

I'm sure that some of you might be saying, "Hey, Bob, you can't be nice to everyone; some people are downright mean." Well, I suppose that there could be some validity to that. Certainly there are some people I have met that I would rather have just smacked. But I am also quite sure that for every one of them, there is probably one who has met me and probably thought that I deserved a good kick in the pants! I have a feeling that most of us would not want to keep a scorecard in that department.

So the way I figure, we should try to be especially nice to those who seem unkind. They probably need it more than anyone else. And maybe deep down inside they really aren't an unkind person. I know that sometimes I've been preoccupied or having a tough day, and I could have possibly given someone the wrong impression.

It's too easy to become preoccupied with ourselves. But that doesn't mean that it is acceptable to do so. Earlier on, I talked about my time in the rehab hospital and how I really cared only about myself. It's not as if I completely ignored everyone, but with the exception of probably two people, I didn't want to listen to anybody else's problems. After all, I was there to get better, not to make friends, right? Well, that probably wasn't such a great plan. Of course I was there to get better, but would it have killed me to show a little compassion to someone who was hurting? You would have thought so at the time. I think that my accident and injury hardened my heart just a little. Or, perhaps, more than a little.

I can say without a doubt that it was Sharon's illness that was the true turning point in my life, both emotionally and spiritually. While I remained focused on Sharon's condition and on her care, it was almost as if God tapped me on the shoulder and said, "I have some other things for you to do as well." Other patients and their families began seeking Sharon and me out to talk with us. They were going through a difficult time (as we were) and were obviously looking for guidance. I guess we looked as if we had a handle on things and could possibly give some positive insight as to what was ahead of them.

Perhaps this is why we had to become stronger. Other people were going to be coming to us in search of strength. And one thing that I know without a doubt is that you cannot fill up somebody else's bucket if yours is empty. We needed to become a fountain of strength, as it was obvious that we needed to share a little bit of it with others.

It was a special time for me as I came full circle from my days in the hospital with my hey-I've-got-problems-of-my-own attitude. It felt good to make a difference to someone.

And it doesn't necessarily have to be something

big that you do. Sometimes even a smile or just a kind gesture can make a difference to someone. I always try to avoid making empty gestures. All too often people say that they will "keep a person in their thoughts."

I know that they mean well, but that doesn't work for me. It's too easy to say that and then forget about it. I began the practice of actually writing the person's name down.

It often astounds people. They will be telling me about a family member, and I'll ask for the person's name and then add it to my list. It's the only way that I will remember and be able to keep my word. And if I tell someone I'm going to pray for them or for someone close to them, I mean it. If you do something enough, it becomes a habit.

So for the next thirty days, smile and say hello to every person you pass. If you see someone that needs a hand with something, lend them a hand instead of walking past them. For the next thirty days, treat everyone you meet as if they are important. They are. The results will astound you, and I bet you will get to the point where you do it without thinking about it (and it will be genuine).

Sure, some people will look at you like you are crazy. It seems that somehow we have evolved to a point where people almost expect rude behavior. People don't communicate with one another the way they used to. Behavior that is less than appropriate is constantly displayed, and glorified for that matter, on television. And of course there is that growing segment of the population that spends every waking hour wearing music earphones or one of those little blinking phone things in their ears. They may not even notice if you do something nice. Many are in their own little world. Many people seldom pay attention to one another anymore. I guess that is just one of the downsides of technology.

No doubt, you will catch some people off guard if you are nice, and they won't know what to make of it. And some may even think that you want something. That's all right. One of the paradoxical commandments of leadership states, *If you do good, people will question your motives. Do good anyway.* So we reach the ones that we are able to reach and make a difference where we can.

This makes me think of a story I once heard about a man walking on the beach.

Thousands of starfish had washed up, and he was throwing them back into the water before the sun would scorch them. A second man who was observing this questioned the first man, who explained what he was doing.

The second man said, "But there are thousands of them. Do you really think you can make a difference?"

The first man replied, "Ask the ones I just threw back if I made a difference."

I think that one of the challenges that exists is that, for those of us who are goal oriented and driven by results, we want to know that we are making a difference. But sometimes we have to just do the right thing, run on faith, and not worry about keeping score. A few years ago a local mechanic that I knew passed away suddenly. Months later when I was talking with his girlfriend, she thanked me for always being a friend to him. I was a little dumbfounded as she explained how he always spoke highly of me and always felt just a little bit better if I stopped by the shop. I never realized that I had made an impact on this man, and to be truthful, it's not something that I ever made a conscious effort to do. The fact that I found out about it is just one of those serendipities in life. I guess my point is that I simply did what I did because it was the right thing to do, not because I was expecting any results. And if I had to live that time over again, I would do it the same even if I wouldn't know the outcome.

After all, are we doing the right thing so we look good, or are we doing it because it is the right thing to do? A man that Sharon knows has been active in the community for many decades and has done many great things for various organizations. And with everything that he has done, there has always been one string attached. If anyone ever puts his picture or his name in the newspaper, they have gotten their last favor. He doesn't do things for the accolades; he does them because it's good to do what is right.

It would be naïve of me to think that any of us are going to change the world on our own. But it doesn't mean that we should not attempt to make a difference along the way.

Maybe we can make a difference in our little corner of it. Try it some time. It's not so bad. All we can do is try to do the right thing and love people, and maybe they'll love us back. And if they don't, well, I just use the other Irish prayer:

> May those who love us, love us and those who
> don't love us, may God turn their hearts and if
> he doesn't turn their hearts may he turn their
> ankles so we'll know them by their limping.

Sounds fair enough. Except that it makes me wonder why *my* ankles are turned and I limp badly. I guess I better not go there!

The *You* in Your Health Care

In addition to the life and spiritual lessons Sharon and I have learned, we have gotten quite an education in the ways of medicine. One of the driving forces behind the writing of this book was the need to share some of what we have learned about navigating around some of the issues we have encountered in the health-care system. Between my days as an EMT working fire and ambulance, having medical professionals in the family, and my direct exposure as a result of some of the abuse my body has taken, medical care is not a foreign topic to me. And, as Sharon had a few health issues prior to the Guillain-Barré illness, she is no stranger to medicine either.

In some ways I am jealous of those people that have never had an illness or injury, but on the other hand, it was the exposure to so many things over the years that allowed me to act in a knowledgeable manner when Sharon got sick. It's very helpful to know the difference between a cat and a CAT scan! Doesn't one of them use a litter box?

The health-care industry has evolved in leaps and bounds over the years. Advances in technology and research have allowed medical care professionals to more accurately diagnose and treat any illness and injury, often with minimal invasion to the body.

Thank goodness, no more drilling and letting the evil spirits out!

We all live in a great time when it comes to the care that is available to us. Sharon and I have been blessed to have had some of the most gifted surgeons work on both of us. From the surgical teams that rebuilt me after my accident; the awesome vascular surgeon who handled Sharon's carotid artery procedure; the doctors at Jefferson, Saint Agnes, and Bryn Mawr Rehab; to the nurses and therapists who worked diligently with us, we are forever in their debt. We truly owe them our lives, and I mean that from the bottom of my heart.

But then I also see some dark ominous clouds looming on the horizon when it comes to medical care. By no means is this meant to sound as if I am "bashing" anyone. I'm not. But it is just a simple fact that there have been a few times where the outcome could have been radically different if we had not stood our ground and spoken up.

The Last Line of Defense

What is the last line of defense, you ask? We are—all of us. All of us that have been patients, will be patients, or have family and loved ones that will be in need of medical care. Oftentimes it is simply a matter of asking the right questions that can mean the difference between life and death.

Years ago Uncle Edward, when talking about

dealing with doctors, stressed the importance of remembering that *medicine is a business!* And I believe that this is a concept that many people forget. And remember, my Uncle Edward was a surgeon. He knew the score as well as anyone. When you get right to the bottom of it all, the truth is that some may have gotten a C+ on the final exam while others were at the top of their class.

We've all heard the joke "What do you call a person who graduated medical school at the bottom of their class? Doctor!" The problem is that when you see all of those diplomas on the wall in the doctor's office, they don't say where he or she ranked! All you know is that they passed. And even if someone was top of the class, it doesn't mean that they have compassion.

Now before anybody starts getting defensive, let me restate that Sharon and I have both dealt with some of the doctors that were obviously top of their class. They are truly gifted and caring people. But we have also dealt with some health care folks that were—well—let's just say I believe that somewhere along the way they lost their ability to care, to be compassionate, and to listen.

I believe that some of them came to exist in what I refer to as a "cookie-cutter" world.

When something didn't fit the mold, they dismissed it. And had we not stood our ground, Sharon may not be here, and I wouldn't be writing this. I had mentioned early on about the episode with Sharon's carotid arteries. She was a stroke just waiting to happen. But since she didn't fit the profile for that type of condition (she was way too young), that doctor initially tried to talk us into letting it ride. But we wouldn't let up.

The first neurologist to examine Sharon with the Guillain-Barré Syndrome flat out stated that it wasn't a big deal. Well, I can tell you that permanent paralysis is a big deal to us, as we both live with it. The inability to breathe on her own, necessitating being on a ventilator for three months, was a big deal to Sharon. It scared the daylights out of me too. Not a big deal? What was this lady thinking? The truly frightening thought that runs through my mind is that every day she continues to treat patients. I can only hope that she has learned a little from our experience.

From that day on, I can assure you that everybody's feet were held to the fire. I cannot stress enough to you the importance of asking questions and holding people accountable. Fortunately, once Sharon was transferred to Jefferson then Saint Agnes and finally Bryn Mawr Rehab, it was smooth sailing.

But I continued to watch and listen, everyone and everything. And so did Sharon. Unfortunately, there was that communications barrier. But believe me, her hearing worked. I think that sometimes people forget that just because someone is paralyzed and on life support, it doesn't mean that they aren't aware of what is going on. At one point, a student nurse had been in Sharon's hospital room, and as this sweet young girl was leaving, she commented to a nurse, "You know, I just don't understand this woman; all she does, day in and day out, is lay there and do nothing." We laugh about it now, but Sharon later told me that at the time, all she could think was, *Sweetheart, if I could rise up out of this bed, you would never grow another hair on your head again.* All right then, message received, over and out. Yes, Sharon can be direct at times.

But overall, those three facilities and the staff members there get high marks. It was actually at those facilities where I learned an invaluable lesson regarding patient advocacy and the involvement of family members in patient care. Good health care providers will welcome the involvement of family in patient care, but the great ones *expect* it. I honestly believe that. I recall that one of the nurses we worked with took an extremely strong stand on this. Her position with family members was simply, "You better learn how to take care of this person because I won't be going home with you!"

She made families get involved. That's how it should be.

I'm not sure what causes some to resent questions or suggestions, perhaps ego. I don't know. But at the three facilities mentioned, we were dealing with the best of the best. Ann and I stayed involved in every step of Sharon's care, and we felt welcome doing it. We were dealing with a lot of people who possessed the ability to check their ego at the door.

I recall one episode where Sharon was not tolerating certain medications. She was so sick and nothing was helping. Finally, I asked the doctor if it was possible to try one other medication that I suggested by name. My reason was the difference in the manner that the medication could be administered. I felt that it was at least worth a try as long as there would not be any adverse effects with any of the other medications that Sharon was already taking. The doctor thought for a minute and decided that it was a great idea. And it worked! But the best part was that he was open to suggestions and always fostered a team mentality.

I guess that the end result of all of this is that Sharon and I no longer blindly accept everything and everyone at face value. Someone may have the diploma, but they are going to have to earn our trust. Sharon and I have been treated well by some of the best and have been blindsided by some of the others. Believe me when I tell you that we will do everything in our power to keep from letting it happen again.

Sharon and I recently had the opportunity to speak to a class of physical-therapy students. The professor was Margie Roos, who had been my physical therapist years ago. We felt truly honored that Margie valued our thoughts and opinions enough to have us speak to her class. It was an enlightening experience in many ways. As I was looking at approximately two-dozen students, I was trying to envision each of them as a therapist and found myself thinking, *I wonder who will make it and who won't. I wonder which ones will become great physical therapists.*

Well, it was almost as if Sharon were reading my

mind (watch it, fellas; wives can do that, you know). Sharon had been talking about some of the positive experiences she had with her therapist Megan, and then she said something very profound. She said, "I'm sure you are sitting there wondering what we are bringing to you, but, as I sit here, I wonder how many "Megans" there are in this room today."

We soon found our answer. We found our answer in those that kept their attention riveted to us. When I made the statement regarding good health-care professionals welcoming family involvement but great ones expecting it, we had our answer. When I repeated it so they could write it down, I saw five hands writing.

When the class was over, everyone got up and left, except five gals who chose to stay and talk one-on-one with us. They wanted to learn more. They weren't interested in being average. They wanted to understand more from a patient's perspective. These are the kind of people Sharon and I want to deal with when we are sick.

I have no doubt that there were probably a few students that we didn't make an impact on. How do I know that? Because the law of averages says so. Also, the glazed look in a few of their eyes was a dead giveaway. But if something Sharon or I said that day made a difference to even one student there, then it was time well spent. And it would appear that we stirred something in the minds of at least five of them. Good odds, I would say. While Sharon and I always welcome the opportunity to share our story and its lessons, our goal in speaking with the students was very clear cut. Through our story they can learn things that are not in any textbook, understanding not only what the patient is thinking but also what family members or advocates are dealing with. Sharon and I believe that the sooner these ideas are indoctrinated, the more successful the students will be throughout their careers.

There just isn't enough that I can say regarding patient advocacy. While I believe that overall the system works, the truth is that perfection doesn't exist. It would be foolish to think that perfection is possible. And so the solution is that we, as either the patient or the advocate, need to be the last line of defense. We need to speak up, ask questions, and make sure that people are held accountable.

By now, I have no doubt that a few people are thinking, *Wait a minute; I'm not going to challenge my doctor or a nurse.* And I'm saying, "Why not?" Do all of those diplomas on the wall intimidate you? That's all right; they used to intimidate me too. Sure I respect my doctors and the education they have received. And I have a special place in my heart for all of the wonderful nurses who have cared for Sharon and me over the years. But I also know that they put their pants on one leg at a time just as I do. They are people, just like you and me.

And I think that it makes more sense to speak to them straight up and on the level and ask intelligent questions to make sure everyone is on the same page. Then we can work together as a team and achieve the desired results: good health care and patient safety. We all owe it to ourselves.

The Best Customer Is an Educated Customer

I'm not really sure who coined that phrase, but I have heard it countless times and believe it to be true. We live in what many refer to as the "information age," a time when we can acquire information on just about any topic in mere seconds.

But somehow many of us go through life and know very little about health and about our bodies. I will be the first to admit that I never made a point of learning about medicine and the human body. It was more by happenstance, although it may be more appropriate to say that it was by "accident," as I learned more than I ever would have imagined after I turned an airplane into a lawn dart.

While I have stressed the importance of patient advocacy, the only way to be an effective advocate is to know what to ask and what to look for. And most of us don't.

Perhaps there was a time when we could simply run on blind faith, but Sharon and I don't see that as an option anymore.

There are things about human nature that I find amazing. We are all funny creatures. In some ways we can be very demanding, and we expect the biggest bang for our buck. There are countless consumer-oriented publications that allow us to do side-by-side comparisons on all sorts of products.

Whether we are buying a refrigerator, plasma television, or a new car, we compare statistics to make sure we get the best product. And we often spend more time than is reasonable doing it. After all, it's our money, right? Believe me, I have certainly done this countless times myself. How many times do we question what a contractor or repairman tells us? We question a seventy-five dollar part for our car and in fact often ask for the old parts. After all, that is what the so-called experts say we should do to make sure we are not getting ripped off.

But then our doctors tell us we need a test, a procedure, a new prescription, or a revised prescription, and so often many of us simply say okay. Trusting souls, aren't we? Trusting with the most valuable asset we have, our bodies. I realize that frequently we don't know what questions to ask. And we certainly don't want to ask a silly question and appear ignorant, do we? Well, I can tell you that I have yet to be laughed at for asking a question, at least not to my face! Either way, I really don't care.

And when all else fails, the one thing I have applied to many situations is to ask one simple question—*does it make sense?* Sometimes logic can go a long way over technical data. Referring back to Sharon's diagnosis, everything that was being said just wasn't making sense. The doctors were sticking with the idea of low potassium as if it were the "magic-bullet theory." The idea of low potassium causing total paralysis did not make sense to me at all. My only regret is that I backed off and didn't lean on them harder.

The lesson here is that your gut rarely lies to you.

Sharon and I continue to strive to learn as much as we can so we can ask the right questions. After all, we are talking about our health here. And if we have questions, we will ask them. If something doesn't make sense, we clarify it.

We had no choice but to change providers since the infamous Guillain-Barré incident, as we wanted to maintain a relationship with some of those that had worked with Sharon throughout her recovery. At the recommendation of my sister Maryanne, a nurse for three decades, and her husband, Greg, who is a doctor, we have teamed up with a new practice that we are extremely happy with. But I will tell you that before we bothered to have all of our records sent over to the new practice, we got to know them first. The first time I called, the receptionist wanted to send us release forms for the records transfer. All I said was, "Hey, let's all dance one dance together and see how we like each other." If for some reason we didn't think this group was what we were looking for, then we would have continued searching. But there was no need.

I absolutely view the patient-doctor relationship as just that: a relationship. I cannot overstate the need for all of us to develop a working relationship with our doctors and the need to educate ourselves.

And there is no time like the present. Waiting until you or a loved one is gravely ill is not the time to start educating oneself. After all, would you wait until you were thirsty to dig the well?

The Insurance Maze

The topic of health insurance has become one of the most highly debated lately. The cost of medical care has risen dramatically, driving increases in insurance rates, making coverage costly. The prices of prescription medications are through the ceiling, causing many people to have to make some very tough financial choices.

Meanwhile, pharmaceutical companies are posting outrageous profits and are engaging in what I would term, at best, questionable business practices in order to amass those profits. The United States Department of Justice (DOJ) apparently takes an even stronger view on these actions.

A February 2008 news release as well as a posting in the DOJ Web site told of Merck Pharmaceuticals agreeing to pay more than $650 million in fines for alleged fraud involving failure to pay rebates to Medicaid. The allegations state that the company failed to pay proper rebates to Medicaid and other government health-care programs and paid illegal remuneration to health-care providers to induce them to prescribe the company's products.[2] The suit specifically mentioned two drugs: Zocor, a cholesterol-lowering drug, and Vioxx, used to treat acute arthritis pain, which was pulled from the market in 2004. Merck allegedly offered steep discounts if hospitals used large quantities in place of competitors' brands, while failing to report these prices to the government as required by law in the Medicaid Rebate Statute. Hmm—I'm shocked.

Long story short, while there was no admission of guilt, an agreement was reached to pay the fine. In addition, the whistleblower, a former Merck employee, is reported to have received $44.6 million from the federal portion of the settlement and $23.5 million from the state portion. Yes, you read it correctly, *million!* I really think that I need to learn how to whistle.

What does all of this have to do with anything? That's your money; it's our money. It is money that people have paid in outrageous prescription costs and co-pays that keeps stockholders happy, CEOs fatter, and health insurance costs high. Please allow me to be clear on one thing—I am in no way opposed to any company making profits or even as I referred to it, outrageous profits, if it is done ethically. And that is the big stipulation here. I believe in the free enterprise system; I believe that capitalism is a great thing. Our economy is based on it, and we all benefit from it.

However, it isn't just about those that are paying for prescriptions. It is also the taxpayers' money, as Medicaid is funded through tax dollars. By failing to abide by the Medicaid Rebate Statute, it would seem to me that companies like this basically reach into the pocket of every American taxpayer. And this is just one example of what is happening in the industry.

It is no wonder that people have become fixated on prescription costs when choosing insurance plans. But I would be remiss if I didn't share something that we learned when Sharon became gravely ill. A few years back, for reasons I do not recall, we changed insurance carriers. The broker that Sharon spoke with really stressed the value of having good in-hospital coverage. He said that quite often people choose a plan with the best prescription coverage, as that is what is foremost in their minds. I certainly understand that, as our monthly prescription co-pays could choke a grizzly bear, on top of already high insurance premiums.

However, the silver lining in this cloud is that when Sharon was hospitalized for five months, the total cost was covered by the insurance company. To put this in perspective, let me give a brief list of what I am referring to:

- Emergency room and preliminary tests
- Admission and overnight stay
- Helicopter transport to Jefferson Hospital ($10,000 alone)
- Five and a half weeks in intensive care, plasmapheresis and IVIG treatments, blood transfusions, surgical procedures for feeding tube and tracheotomy, and related care, respiratory therapists, daily lab work, etc.

- Transport to Saint Agnes Hospital
- Seven and a half weeks of acute care and weaning off of life support, respiratory therapists, physical and occupational therapists
- Transport to Bryn Mawr Rehab
- Seven weeks of intense physical and occupational therapy and all related medical issues

It's a very abbreviated list, but you get the idea. It was extremely expensive. I was told by one of the hospital staff that the IVIG (intravenous immune globulins) treatments alone were six figures. There were five of those treatments to replace the bad antibodies that were flushed out during the plasmapheresis. Now you might be thinking, what are the chances of ever needing all of that? I hope you will not. But if the need ever arises, I can tell you that the numbers are staggering, and the cost of most people's homes would not come close to covering it.

My point of telling you all of this is that for those who are in a position to shop for their own insurance coverage, or if given choice of plans through one's employer, choose wisely. A policy with good in-hospital coverage is worth its weight in gold. I must say that the idea of low prescription co-pays looked very attractive at the time we were looking at policies, and I am glad that I didn't make the final call. Sharon gets all the credit on this one.

Unfortunately, I don't have a magic wand that can fix the current health-care crisis. If I did, just perhaps I would be running for president. Well, a sharp blow to the head would probably be a prerequisite as well. While some believe that socialized medicine is the answer, I do not. Now I swore that I would not get political in this book, but some days I just can't help myself. There is just something about the word *socialized* that just sounds too much like *socialism*. Gee, come to think of it, I think there might be a connection.

But putting the political sarcasm aside, I have serious doubts regarding a total health-care system being run by the folks in Washington. When I look at the lack of efficiency that takes place on a daily basis with wasteful spending, do we all really want or need the federal government overseeing our health?

When we get right down to the nitty-gritty of the idea, we must take a long hard look at other programs that the government has run and has had financial oversight of and ask ourselves two very sobering questions. The first question is have those programs been run with operational efficiency and responsibility? (Do they work?) The second question is have those programs been run with fiscal efficiency and responsibility?

Actually, it is the answers that are sobering, because in my humble opinion, the answer to the first question is *no, not really,* and the answer to the second question is an emphatic *no, not all.* I think you see where I am headed.

Let's look at it another way. Suppose you hire a contractor to overhaul a bathroom and put a new roof on your house. And when it's all said and done, the job costs more than quoted, and the work is poorly done. The first time you flush the toilet, it overflows, the roof leaks every time that it rains, and you can't get him to fix the problems. Do you really want to hire this chap to now overhaul your kitchen? Let us take it one step further. Suppose Congress passes a law mandating that you *must* use this contractor. I know I'd be saying, "Hey, man, it's my kitchen and it's my money, and your guy is the pits. Take a hike!" Do you see what I'm talking about? It's our money, our bodies, and I still think that we should have some say in how we take care of them.

We live in a tax-based society, and I think that people forget one very undeniable fact. And that is that the government cannot give *to* us what it doesn't first take *from* us. And no doubt, they will take far more than is required to run things. History has proven that. The picture that comes to my mind is horror that even the best science-fiction writers could not conjure up. There has never been a time in my life when I would have favored socialized medicine, but the episode of Sharon's Guillain-Barré Syndrome solidified my beliefs.

Although our current system is definitely in need of a tune-up, the fact remains that I was able to get what Sharon needed without having to jump through a series of hoops. I cannot begin to imagine what the outcome would have been if I had needed to wait for bureaucratic red tape to get Sharon flown to a suitable hospital able to treat her illness, let alone get the treatments she needed. Sure, a few procedures needed approval, but it was a matter of a phone call and not a congressional hearing.

In some ways, I kind of equate government-run health care to going to a wedding reception. At such an event, you eat and drink what is being served because someone else is paying your bar tab! Don't think that government-run health care won't have strings attached to it. We already have elected officials trying to put restrictions on what we eat. Sure, I know that too much of anything will really do a number on any of us, but do we really need Congress enacting laws telling us how big of a T-bone we're allowed to order? Some of these clowns have already talked about proposing bills that would limit portion sizes in restaurants, and in a few cities it will be required for restaurants to post nutritional information on menus. I know that the twenty-pound brontosaurus rib rack is not good for me and that I shouldn't order it. So I don't. It's comes down to personal accountability, my friends.

Don't think for a minute that Big Brother won't be in your business even more if "he" is handling your health care. Remember, watch what you wish for, because you just might get it. And then there is no turning back. I, for one, feel quite confident that I am smart enough to take care of myself and make the right choices medically without involving my congressman. Think about it.

Taking Care of Ourselves (Or Not)

Few things in this world amaze me more than the human body. God really created something incredible when he created us. I have always marveled not only at the complexities and intricacies of the human body but also its resiliency. But sometimes we push that resiliency to the limits.

Over the years I have seen a lot of stupid acts committed all in the name of vanity and bravado. And I would be telling a bold-faced lie if I said that I didn't commit a few of those acts. Just watch a car full of guys some time. Actually any type of vehicle will do. Make it a car, boat, or even a bicycle; it doesn't matter. Usually the last thing the driver says is, "Hey, watch this!" That is, of course, just prior to the crash. Ah yes, there is nothing like pushing the limits to look tough.

I have bent a few automobiles, skidded out on a motorcycle or two, broken a few bones along the way, and of course the ultimate finish, crashed an airplane. Some were just accidental; some were a result of stupidity. Believe me, you cannot safely see where you are driving when you're busy trying to see how cool you are! It just doesn't work.

Day after day, week after week, and year after year, people still continue to abuse their bodies, and much of it is by choice. It is hard enough just dealing with the everyday health issues that result from accidents or illnesses. But then we have the growing segment of our population that is bound and determined to put their health at risk. Every year Americans spend billions of dollars on cosmetic surgery procedures, injections of chemicals and various other fillers that paralyze muscles and reduce lines, all in an effort to convince the rest of society that we are younger and sexier than we are. Umm, why?

Now I have to say that I never really paid much attention to any of this until I learned of a lady who was in the hospital at the same time Sharon was. HIPAA laws prevent me from divulging any details, other than the fact that this lady had a severe reaction to some injections she had gotten in an attempt to look younger and as a result ended up on life support. To say that she was depressed would be an understatement.

And this is not the only one of these cases I have since heard of. It hardly seems worth it to me, because it is really hard to look years younger with paralysis and a tracheotomy. Yeah, I know it doesn't happen to everyone, but it's definitely not a gamble I would take. In the words of Sharon's friend Sandy, "I've worked real hard for these lines in my face, and I'm not giving them up!"

Anybody who has ever had any medical procedure done has had to read and sign forms indicating the risks. Have you ever *really* read it closely? When I had a simple hernia surgery, one of the possible risks listed was *death!* It really instills confidence, doesn't it? But I couldn't spend the rest of my life with my insides trying to pop out, so naturally I had to have the surgery and accept those risks.

But for the life of me, I will never understand

when people voluntarily put themselves at risk needlessly. And that is not even taking into account all of those bitten by the tattoo and piercing bug. Call me a pansy, but there is just something about the idea of some guy named "Animal" with pictures all over his body and a bolt through his nose injecting ink into my skin while drawing a picture that gives me the willies. Thanks, but no thanks!

It's difficult enough dealing with all of the things that crop up as simply part of going through life, without going out of our way to look for trouble. I am not saying that people should live their lives in a bubble. After all, nobody is getting out alive in the end. By all means, have fun and enjoy life. But try and be smart about it.

I had the bright (not!) idea to take an airplane to a company picnic and put myself in a situation that I otherwise would not have. What the heck was I thinking? Were my coworkers going to like me better because I took them for airplane rides? Was I going to look cool? They all turned their backs on me anyway. Was it worth it? No, not at all. Am I bitter? No, just smarter now.

In a few short seconds, I went from big man on campus to little man in a body cast. I know that pain is pain and paralysis is paralysis, regardless of how you got there. But I can tell you firsthand that knowing you played a part in getting there just really makes you want to kick yourself in the butt. Of course you can't do that when you have paralysis. So if anybody wants to volunteer to gift me swift kick in the pants, I believe I've got it coming.

All I am saying, friends, is that God has given each of us a great gift, and we need to take care of that gift. Sure, stuff happens. But before we all run out and get nipped, tucked, injected, tattooed, or try something like skateboarding off of the Hoover Dam (or taking an airplane to the company picnic), we need to ask ourselves, is it *really* worth it? Not to say that flying is unsafe, it's just that it is incredibly unforgiving if things go wrong.

The one sure thing that Sharon and I have learned is that we are not at the playground. In real life, when things go bad, you can't say, "Do over," as we all did when we were kids. God has given us all something wonderful, and we need to be good stewards of that which we have been given.

God and Family

The Bible tells us, "With God, all things are possible" (Matthew 19:26), and I don't believe that truer words have ever been spoken. Sharon and I would not be together, and we certainly would not have survived the challenges that we have faced without God's love and blessings.

I guess I would say that my relationship with God officially began in the summer of 1961, when I was baptized at Queen of the Holy Rosary Catholic Church in Overland Park, Kansas. I was actually born in Missouri, but we lived just over the line on Tomahawk Drive in Prairie Village, Kansas. I am the fourth in a line-up of nine children, and from the earliest times that I remember, Mom and Pop always stressed the importance of prayer and that of living a life that was in accordance with God's laws.

My time in the Midwest was short-lived, as the family moved east to Pennsylvania by the time I was five years old. Before long, we were in Concordville at the house on Scott Road, and Mom and Pop had us enrolled at Saint Thomas the Apostle in nearby Chester Heights. It was a great sacrifice on their part to put nine children through Catholic elementary and high school, as those were some lean times. But it was important that we received a proper education as well as learned about God and about strengthening our faith. I look back on that era with great fondness.

I remember that as children we would kneel down and say our prayers together at bedtime. We always had a long list of things that we prayed for. We went to church every Sunday together, as a family, although it took more than one vehicle to get us all there as the family grew. We ate meals together as a family and asked God for his blessings before each meal. In those days, the concept of doing things as a family unit carried great importance. Ultimately, all of these things that we did served as a deep foundation for me to build my faith in God, as well as appreciate family unity. It was in striving to follow these ideals that a foundation was laid to deal with life and its adversities.

I am often taken aback when I hear some individual say they don't believe that God exists. Certainly everyone is free to believe as they wish, but when I look at all of the beauty that surrounds us, I have a difficult time accepting that belief. It is my firm belief that Sharon and I would not be where we are if it were not for God's blessings. I think that we are strong people, but I know that we're not strong enough to make it alone. Sharon's illness was a pivotal point in our lives, as well as a defining moment spiritually. I kept my Bible at Sharon's bedside while she was hospitalized, and I found it to be a great source of strength and inspiration. As I read various passages from the Bible, I found hope. Sure, I had read from the Bible before, but this was different. I felt God's power. Sharon has said that when she was completely paralyzed, she would pray for strength and for a sense of inner peace. I believe that I was feeling that same inner peace.

God had our undivided attention! And despite everything that was happening to Sharon, I wasn't coming apart at the seams. Of course doubt and fear would try to visit once in a while. I recall one night in particular when I sat looking up at the stars asking God to take the illness away or at least to let me have it so that Sharon wouldn't suffer. I couldn't understand why Sharon had to suffer so much, and I couldn't bear the daily pain of watching her. But then again, I have yet to find where it is written that we are supposed to understand. But later that night I found my answer in a Gospel reading and realized that I was only being human.

Jesus was in the Garden of Gethsemane, knowing that in just a few hours He would be betrayed and put to death. Jesus said, "Father, if it is Your will, take this cup away from Me; nevertheless not My will, but Yours, be done" (Luke 22:42).

I found great strength in that verse. Even Jesus had His human side and was not asking for anything unreasonable. After all, would a sane person gladly accept such a fate? I was simply trying to find answers, which is often easier said than done. But I realized that we had to accept God's will.

We often search for answers, but when we don't get the answers that we are looking for, it is easy to think that God isn't listening to us. What a silly bunch we are; God always listens! But at times the answers are not so obvious. Sometimes God has other plans for us. And as painful as the idea might seem, we occasionally have to use our heads and figure out solutions. The answers aren't always handed to us.

One day someone faxed me a little verse that reads as follows:

Answer to Prayers

We ask God for strength and God gives us difficulties to make us strong.

We pray for wisdom and God sends us problems, the solution of which develops wisdom.

We plead for prosperity and God gives us brain and brawn to work.

We plead for courage and God gives us dangers to overcome.

We ask for favors and God gives us opportunities.

This is the answer.

- Author unknown

This reminds me of when I was young. Whenever I or any of my siblings would go to my father with a question, he never gave us the answer outright. He always made us think it through. I would ask a question, and he would ask me what I thought the solution was. Now, what was running through my mind was, *Gee Pop, if I knew the solution, do you think I would have asked you?* So I would go think it through and come back with what I felt was a good solution, and then we would discuss that.

The point is that he challenged us to think and to use what resources we had to figure out solutions to problems. And for that I am grateful. Thanks, Pop! It was all of those mental exercises and my spiritual upbringing that has enabled me to think and solve problems and to continue to change and try to evolve into a better person. Just as God doesn't always give the answer we are looking for, neither did my father. It was great training to be able to deal with life.

Certainly I wish that Sharon had not become gravely ill, and I wish that I had not been in the airplane accident. If I were to say otherwise, I think that would make me either a liar or a fool, or perhaps both. But I cannot deny that these experiences have forced me to become a different person. Looking back, I can see that I *needed* to change. And the only way to make a change for the better is through God. It means that we will have to stretch and grow a little or, as in my case, maybe a lot. But we can always make the journey as long as we remember that God is leading us.

In 1990 I came pretty close to the edge, and in 2006 Sharon came closer than I care to think about. We both have had the grim reaper knocking at our door. Fortunately for both of us, it wasn't our time. But the experiences have changed us in many ways. Now don't worry, I'm not going to start telling you how the grass is greener or how the chirping of the birds sounds sweeter. The grass is the same color, and the birds sound the same. Believe me.

But I will share a few thoughts with you from the heart. Our experiences have opened our eyes to just how important we are to each other, to what's really going on around us, and how we, collectively as a society, have lost sight of our priorities.

I feel quite fortunate to have grown up when and where I did and to have been raised by parents that taught me the right way to live. Mom and Pop made great sacrifices in those early years. Money was not plentiful, and if I said that we all walked to school and it was uphill both ways, it would make for a great country song. But actually, we only walked uphill to the bus stop, and it really was downhill coming the other way! So I feel a little spoiled.

Some families I knew had a vacation property at the beach. Some had in-ground swimming pools. We did not. We had a piece of land, a big old farm house, a barn, and a pond full of fish, snakes, and snapping turtles, which we used to swim in all the time.

What did we know?

We had this big old Case tractor, and long before I could start it, I knew how to hitch up and operate the plow. You see, it had one of those hand cranks in the front as the old cars did, and I was a pretty small kid and didn't have enough muscle to crank it without help. We worked hard. We played hard too.

So while other kids were basking in the sun at the beach all summer, we worked (and swam with all the snapping turtles!). And while a lot of other kids went to the local schools, Mom and Pop really learned how to stretch a dollar (Mom could squeeze a nickel until the buffalo went "mooo") to send us to good schools. While our studies were a priority, we all played sports and worked, as well as volunteered at the hospital and the local fire company. Mom and Pop had instilled into us all a sense of giving back to the community. Is this sounding like a country song yet?

All right, a few times the tractor didn't start, and our goat died. Now it's a country song! But I can honestly say from the bottom of my heart that if I had to live those years over, I would do it the way we did. Looking back, the funny part is that other kids thought we were the ones that had money. Perspective is an interesting thing.

My point to all of this is simply that my siblings and I learned how to work together and play together. We backed up one another going into burning buildings to fight fires. And that wasn't just the guys. My sisters weren't above strapping on an airpack and dragging a hose into a burning building. We learned how to live together as a family, how to love one another, and yes, even how to squabble with one another on occasion.

But equally as important, we learned how to get over our differences, still respect one another, and move on.

Jack and I learned how to do stupid stuff and get

in dutch together. Frankly it amazes me that one of us didn't end up paralyzed at a much younger age. I mean, we pulled some really dumb stunts. And seeing as I'm younger and smaller, I usually felt the greater impact—literally!

Despite all of it, some good times and some times when everyone hasn't seen eye to eye on everything, the fact remains that we are family. And we always will be family.

It causes me great pain when I hear someone say that they have a family member that they haven't spoken to in years. Sometimes people have told me their story about why they aren't speaking to a family member, and quite often it is over something small. Two people simply cannot agree that they disagree and then lose sight of what is really important.

Some of you might be saying, "Sure, Bob, but you don't have my family." That's true, I don't have your family. I have mine, and while I love them dearly, it would be totally unrealistic to think that everyone is going to agree on everything all of the time. I have discovered that the "theory of relativity" actually has nothing to do with science. It states that sometimes family can drive you crazy and that holidays and gatherings can be a real handful once in a while. You heard it here first!

For goodness sake, Sharon and I certainly don't always agree on everything. And I used to do a really good job of being mad for several days. I mean, I was a real pro at it.

And then I almost lost her. It was time to wake

up. I was only making myself look small. It's just not worth sweating the small stuff in life. We all need to hold family and loved ones close to us. They're not cars—you can't trade them in or replace them.

What does all of this have to do with Sharon and me and our near-fatal experiences?

Well, for one thing, I believe that if I had some kind of cushy powder-puff upbringing, I probably would have burst into flames at the slightest adversity. I learned how to be a fighter. Sharon is the oldest of five and didn't exactly grow up in the lap of luxury either.

As a result, she too learned to be a fighter, a survivor. As I've said, "her momma grew her strong."

And the second thing is that in both of our situations, family played a vital role in dealing with our respective traumas. Fortunately, I married a gal who is well grounded, and we both have families that despite any differences there may be (and every family has them), they are willing to jump into the ring when the bell sounds. And Sharon and I would do the same for any of them. These experiences served as reminders as to just how important family is.

What ultimately concerns me is that little by little people are forgetting that, and the family unit is eroding away. So many families exist in such a way that each member is almost its own entity entirely. I don't want to sound as though I am generalizing, as I am not referring to every family. What I am referring to is a trend that I see. The tail is wagging the dog.

Along with the erosion of the family unit has

come an erosion of faith in God, unfortunately in epidemic proportions. And I believe that there is a direct correlation between the two. I'm sure by this point a few politically correct individuals have already set fire to their copy of this book. So be it.

People have lost sight of what is really important. Oftentimes it is easier to do what is popular than what is right. And it's often easy to forget about one another in the process. We, as a society, have lost our focus on one another and become focused on things.

We have become a society that is taking the phrase "keeping up with the Joneses" to excessive levels. Now before you go and think that I am one of those people that believes money is the root of evil, let me stop you. I believe that success and wealth are great things. After all, even the Bible tells us, "And you shall remember the Lord your God, for it is He who gives you the power to get wealth" (Deuteronomy 8:18). I consider that to be a pretty good endorsement.

I believe that money is a wonderful thing, and to be truthful, I rank it right up there next to oxygen. There are just some things that are difficult to do without. And I have seen good people do good things with money. But a disturbing trend has existed for some time now where folks are spending money that they *don't* have to obtain things that don't really matter.

It has become ever so important to have the house with the greatest amount of square footage or the certain brand of automobile that screams "status."

The truly alarming part is that many cannot afford these things and are putting their futures and those of their families in serious jeopardy. For that matter, the economy of our nation has been put in jeopardy as a result of this as well as many other factors. These material things have become more important to people than faith and family. These material things have become their "golden calf," so to speak.

Of all of the bumper stickers I have seen on cars, one of my least favorite has the saying "He who dies with the most toys wins." This has to be one of the greatest lies ever told, right up there with "the check is in the mail." The real truth is that he who dies with the most toys is, nevertheless, dead. All of those things don't fit in a casket, so we can't take them with us. Somehow I have a hard time believing that there are boat slips and airplane hangars in Heaven. Although, just between you and me, I wouldn't mind being wrong on that one!

I am constantly amazed at how people will camp out for several days in a cold, driving rainstorm so their kid can be the first to have the latest video game or cell phone. Would any of us camp out in that weather for several days in order to get our children into a good school? Would we do it to get into church? Somehow I don't envision that happening on any large scale. What has happened to everybody's priorities? I know that Sharon and I have reclaimed ours. There is something about staring death in the face and then climbing from the abyss that causes one to reevaluate what really matters at the end of the day. There is something about almost losing what is most important to us that serves as a great reminder about just what is most important.

As we travel down the road of life, we all need to keep a few simple things in mind. We live in what I believe to be the greatest country in the world. We can have just about anything we want if we are willing to work for it, but we need to remember that happiness lies within our hearts and our minds. We live in a country where we have more rights and freedoms than any others. But I believe that those rights come at a price.

Along with rights come responsibilities.

I believe that we have the responsibility to love and serve God, to love and take care of one another, and to be responsible citizens of this great nation. But most importantly, we have been charged with the task of teaching each new generation to do the same thing.

The rest is simply icing on the cake.

Epilogue

It has been an honor to share our story with you. While it would appear that Sharon is not destined to make a full recovery, she continues to strive each day to make any gains possible. I, of course, reached a plateau years ago. While some may consider the lack of a full recovery for either of us to be an unhappy ending to the story, we don't consider it necessarily to be unhappy or even the end of our story. After all, neither of us is planning to go anywhere yet.

So our journey continues to unfold with each new day. As we look to the future, we see a bright future, primarily because we choose to. Is it easy? Of course it isn't. Each of us has suffered a loss and has had to, in our own way, grieve that loss. But then it is important to move on, take each new day and live it to the fullest, and make a difference where we can.

And while it is our hope that none of you ever go through what Sharon and I have, we know that everyone faces their own hardships in some form or another, their own version of *The Twist in the Road*. After all, as we all know, "stuff" happens to all of us. In fact, during the writing of this book, I have had two family members battle cancer. Fortunately, those battles have been victorious so far. For those that are hitting a rough spot in life, take solace in knowing that our prayers are with you and that we believe that God watches over all of us.

We believe that any of us can accomplish any goal or dream that we have as long as we persevere and have faith in God. And there is no doubt that one may encounter adversity along the way. While many believe that adversity builds character, Sharon and I do not. We believe that adversity *defines* character, both yours and that of those around you. And we have been surrounded by some of the best.

Thank you to all of you wonderful people who have touched our lives along the way and to those of you who have allowed us to touch your lives and hopefully make a difference. God bless you all.

Contact Information

For any questions, comments, or information,
feel free to write to Bob and Sharon at:

120 Richard Road
Aston, PA 19014

or

E-mail to
Bobhanlonbooks@aol.com

End Notes

1. Scott, Foresman Advanced Dictionary (Glen-view, Illinois: Scott, Foresman and Company, 1979) 1168

2. United States Department of Justice, "Merck to Pay More than $650 Million to Resolve Claims of Fraudulent Price Reporting and Kickbacks," United States Department of Justice. http://www.usdoj.gov/opa/pr/2008/February/08_civ_094.html.

Bibliography

Scott, Foresman Advanced Dictionary. Glenview, Illinois: Scott, Foreman and Company, 1979.

United States Department of Justice. "Merck to Pay More than $650 Million to Resolve Claims of Fraudulent Price Reporting and Kickbacks." United States Department of Justice. http://www.usdoj.gov/opa/pr/2008/February/08_civ_094.html.